FOLLOW ME
as I Follow Jesus

A Red-Letter Journey
Through the Gospel of John

Mary Jo Pierce has pitched her tent in the land of hope—the land where the One who calls her Beloved waits to meet with her. The good news for readers is that Mary Jo wants to teach us how to dwell in that land with the One who loves us beyond measure.

With incredible transparency, Mary Jo walks us across the terrain of her life—the places where she waits, trusts, listens, and yields. We hike through crags where hunger and thirst abound and joy is deep and sustaining. Crossing through hills and valleys, she shows us how to surrender quietly and enter into His rest.

Reading *Follow Me as I Follow Jesus*, you will encounter the Lord. You will drink and be satisfied, but you will also want so much more. One of my heroes in the faith, Mary Jo is a forerunner in the prayer pastor movement. Join me in following Mary Jo as she follows Jesus.

HEIDI SCANLON
Pastor of Prayer | National Community Church | Washington DC

Spend only a few moments with Mary Jo Pierce, and you will know you are walking with someone who *lives* the gospel. This remarkable woman is my spiritual mother, and through her writing, she has become a spiritual mother to us all. In a world desperate to hear God's voice and know He is always speaking, *Follow Me as I Follow Jesus* is a true gift. Simply put, Mary Jo shows us how to walk hand in hand with the Savior. Her love for Jesus, His Word, and His voice is contagious!

This book isn't romanticized ideology. It's as practical as the nose on your face. God is a real person who longs to talk to His children. Through her prayer chair, challah bread, and tentology, Mary Jo gives us a tangible picture of what a relationship with God looks like in real life. *Follow Me as I Follow Jesus* will inspire you to lean in, hear God's voice, and enjoy His presence. I should know—I ordered my own prayer chair when I finished reading!

TIFFINI KILGORE
Owner | House of Belonging
Author | Creator | Misfit Table

Gimmicks. Fads. Let's be honest: they "work" for a little while. But after a short season, they run their course and give way to the next one. There is a better, forgotten way—the ancient way. God's people have prayed—really prayed—in ancient ways for thousands of years. Unfortunately, God's people have not been as diligent to train the generations behind them.

That's when God raises up people like Mary Jo Pierce. She bloodied her knuckles on fads and trends and found them wanting. But because she loves God, she held on and re-dug the old wells. And as you read *Follow Me as I Follow Jesus*, she will teach you the ancient ways.

This book is God's call to each of us to learn how to walk with Him. Praying is not the goal. **Praying is how we attach ourselves to God.** Throughout all of human history, God's people have used Scripture to begin speaking with God. This is the ancient, time-tested way of connecting with the Ancient of Days.

Learning to pray is not reserved only for certain people. God is calling **you**.

MARCUS BRECHEEN
Coach at marcusbrecheen.com

I love Mary Jo. She's been a sweet friend for many years. I'm always inspired by her close friendship with Jesus and how knitted she is to the Word of God. This book is anointed to invite you into a new conversation and deeper relationship with the God who loves you so passionately.

KARI JOBE CARNES
Worship Leader | Songwriter

When I think of Mary Jo, I remember how it felt to be in the presence of Corrie Ten Boom as she spoke about the love of God. Within a few moments of Mary Jo's voice shaping words that describe the presence and pursuit of God, one can feel the very thing she speaks of physically hanging in the room. Few people have this gift—it comes only after having spent so much time with God that you find yourself lathered in His presence.

In her first book, *Adventures In Prayer*, Mary Jo taught us how to order a nourishing meal (with prayer being the food). Now in *Follow Me as I Follow Jesus*, she expands the menu. Readers will become hungry for more than just being heard; they will crave constant conversation with the Savior.

I sincerely recommend this book to anyone who desires communion with the Lord. So many people struggle with the belief that they cannot hear His voice. Mary Jo dispels the myth that one must work and do in order to hear or be heard by God. Conversations with Him start as easily as "Hello." One must simply be willing to sit, listen, and obey.

RITA SPRINGER
Founder | DIVE Worship School
Worship Leader | Recording Artist | Author

It's a rare phenomenon when an author strikes the right balance between transparency and deep thought that causes readers to reach their own conclusions. Mary Jo Pierce accomplished this in *Follow Me as I Follow Jesus*.

This in-depth conversation with Jesus will appeal to all your senses, satiate your intellect with solid content, inspire your creativity in hearing God, and challenge you to look at your prayer life from a different perspective. With breathtaking candor, Mary Jo challenges our tired mindset of what prayer should look like. She inspires us to ask God honest questions, listen for answers, and then "follow Him" to a deeper relationship.

Follow Me as I Follow Jesus is full of whimsy, poignant thoughts, and beautifully transparent prayers—a must-read for anyone eager to go deeper in their own prayer life. I found this book to be a rare gem. Be prepared for the wonderful, God-inspired unexpected.

JOANNA WIESINGER, PH.D.
Owner | Thrive with Strengths
Gallup Strengths Coach

MARY JO PIERCE

FOLLOW ME
as I Follow Jesus

A Red-Letter Journey
Through the Gospel of John

beginwithbread.com

Follow Me as I Follow Christ: A Red-Letter Journey Through the Gospel of John
Copyright © 2018, 2025 by Mary Jo Pierce

maryjopierce.com

ISBN: 979-8-9923901-0-0
eBook ISBN: 979-8-9923901-1-7

Design and publishing services by wildcreativepublishing.com

Cover photo of Mary Jo Pierce taken in Capernaum at the Sea of Galilee.

Printed in the United States of America

Holy Spirit,

   Thank You for enlightening me to the wonder and awe of actually stepping into the Scriptures and engaging in a personal, revelatory conversation with Jesus.

Jesus,

   Thank You for taking me by the hand and walking with me from John 1 to John 21—lingering when I needed to, leading me, and loving me all along the way.

Father, the Holy One Blessed Be He,

   Thank You for giving Your only begotten Son, the living Word, that I may live life with Him on earth and follow Him into eternity.

This labor of love and pure joy is humbly and gratefully dedicated.

My God, Three in One
Holy Trinity

CONTENTS

READ THIS FIRST

Imagine being Nicodemus and secretly meeting with Jesus at night. Imagine being the woman at the well and having the Savior ask you for a drink. Imagine being at the Last Supper and having the Messiah wash your feet. Just imagine …

The idea of engaging in a one-on-one conversation with Jesus is certainly thought-provoking. What would it be like to speak with Him face-to-face, heart-to-heart? How would it change you? What would you be willing to give to hear Jesus say, "Come, follow Me"?

⌒m⌒

I've always taken the Word personally. At the inception of my relationship with Jesus, the Word became my friend. Scripture showed me the plans God has for me, acted as a compass for everyday decisions, and served as a measuring rod for my life. The Bible introduced me to the unconditional love of God, marked out how to have relationships, and taught me how to worship, pray, believe, and hope. The Word was my light, truth, and trusted companion.

However, as always with our God, there is more. And when we discover the more, God has even *more.* He is continually revealing more depth and breadth and height and width to His unfailing love, unwavering mercy, and eternal goodness. God is the same yesterday, today, and tomorrow. He doesn't change. His Word doesn't change. No matter how much our situations or circumstances may change, the Bible always can and always will speak to our current state. It's incredible!

In response to my prayer, "I want to get to know Jesus more" (which I will share more about later), God invited me to walk into the Scriptures and have a personal conversation with Jesus by primarily using the red-letter words in the book of John. What I thought would be another assignment turned out to be the most authentic, raw, and transforming encounter I've ever had with Jesus and the Word.

This book will take you on my journey through the Gospel of John and invite you into your own. I'll share from my journals as you write in yours. Together, we will each have our own Emmaus Road, walking and talking with Jesus.

I'm mindful there are verses, words, and thoughts that spoke specifically to what God was wanting to address with me on my journey. There were many conversations in red Jesus did not highlight for me, and those He did may differ from those He will highlight for you. God has specific work He wants to do in and through each of us, and His Word will speak to your life as directly and spot-on as it did to mine.

Starting out, I anticipated this journey to take 21 days (21 chapters, one chapter each day). In truth, I spent a year walking through the Gospel of John with Jesus. In "real" life, conversations ebb and flow, change the subject, later return to the original subject, and so on. The same is true with this journey. This is not a book with a traditional beginning, middle, and end. Rather, it reflects the genuine, day-in and day-out, high and low, mountain top and valley, failing and get up and go again, run the race conversations.

God is so amazingly *personal*. I pray this book unlocks many hearts and begins endless conversations.

In the beginning was the Word, and the Word was with God, and the Word was God. He was in the beginning with God. All things were made through Him, and without Him nothing was made that was made. In Him was life, and the life was the light of men. And the light shines in the darkness, and the darkness did not comprehend it (John 1:1–5 NKJV).

Here are the tools I used:

- A new journal (I love the promise of a new journal—all those blank pages soon to be filled with life lessons and treasures and secrets between God and me.)
- A red pen to indicate Jesus (God) speaking to me
- A blue pen to indicate me speaking to Jesus (God— Sometimes my conversations were with the Father and the Holy Spirit too.)
- Another color pen for sidebar notes, commentary, etc. (optional)
- A Bible (I used The Voice translation. Its script form helped me "step into the story of Scripture," and its added italicized words and phrases drew me into personal conversations with Jesus. I often referenced other translations to add depth and width to our conversations.)

Someone once asked me to name my favorite Bible translation. I replied, "The MJP version"—my initials. In all seriousness, when I find a Bible passage that God wants engraved on my heart, I will read every translation I can find. I then write the Scripture selection in my own words, sometimes including my name or the names of my loved ones. I follow this practice so that I can personally identify with what God is saying to me in that moment.

As I walked and talked with Jesus on this journey, I often found what He was speaking in each chapter to be very pertinent to what was going on in my life at that time. I was able to take His words from their original historical context and apply them directly to my own present circumstances. The wonderful thing about this method of reading and praying Scripture is that if I were to do it again, Jesus' words would be the same, but our conversations would be different. My life is ever-growing, ever-challenging, and ever-seeking. Thankfully, His Word is alive and always applicable to what is going on in my heart *today*.

As much as I consider my red-letter journal to be one of my greatest treasures, my objective is not simply to share my experiences and insights. My greatest desire is for *you* to have your own journey.

> Follow my example, as I follow the example of Christ (1 Corinthians 11:1 NIV).

Many of the prayers I share in this book have blank lines for you to fill in with your own details—your needs, your heartaches, your dreams. Let the Holy Spirit direct and lead you in your own transforming encounter with Jesus. Don't be in a hurry. Walk at a leisurely pace and enjoy your intimate, first person interactions with your Savior.

> Blessed are those who make You their strength,
>   for they treasure *every step of* the journey
>   (Psalm 84:5).

TO KNOW YOU MORE

It was the last few days of November 2012. I was sitting in my prayer room, thinking, "Where has this year gone?" Reflecting on God's faithfulness and how He was having His way in and through my prayer life, I realized there was much to celebrate. The past year had been a busy one, filled with a lot of good things, many great things, and countless God-things. However, something felt unfinished. There was a yearning in my spirit I was attempting to put into words.

Jesus, I *desire* to know You more.

Then a thought.
Perhaps a whisper.
For certain a hunger.

Jesus, I *want* to know You more.
Jesus, I *need* to know You more.

I had long ago come to recognize these ideas and feelings as gifts from God. He was drawing me closer to Him. There was only one question: what would be my response? I immediately thought of this treasured hymn:

And He walks with me and He talks with me
And He tells me I am His own
And the joy we share as we tarry there
None other has ever known.[1]

I began repeating the refrain in my mind until it settled into my spirit.

Then I thought of the term *walking in the Rabbi's dust.*

In Jesus' day young men who wanted to become disciples of a rabbi would leave their families and jobs and follow him. "Walking in his dust" referred to how closely they were to listen and learn as they traveled the dirt roads of Jerusalem. The apostles Peter, Andrew, James, and John were well-acquainted with this type of rabbi-disciple relationship. When Jesus said, *"Come and follow Me"* (Mark 1:17), their response was immediate. They stayed that day and remained with Jesus the rest of their lives.

That's it! I wanted:

- The Emmaus Road experience where my heart would burn with His Word
- To meet Jesus at the well and have an in-depth conversation about spirit and truth
- To sit at His feet like Mary and hear "[she] has chosen the good part" (Luke 10:42 NASB)
- To cry over the city of Jerusalem with Him
- To watch and pray in the Garden of Gethsemane

I wanted to experience Jesus as if I were walking and talking with Him face-to-face. I wanted to cross over to a new place of communion and fellowship. I wanted to reach out and touch Him!

The idea was to *walk* through the pages of the Gospel of John

---

[1] C. Austin Miles, "In the Garden," 1913, Public Domain.

and have a conversation using the red-letter words as if Jesus were speaking directly to me. What a good-great-God idea! 21 chapters. 21 days. Done in time for Christmas, with a few days left before starting my New Year's fast. Or so I thought. But God had other plans …

Several months later, I asked Jesus if He realized we were still at the well (John 4). I sensed His "My plans are not your plans" smile. Only He knew where this Emmaus Road journey would take me and that it would last the remainder of the year.

Well, it's time to get started! Are you ready for your "in the beginning?" As I read John 1:1, 4–5, excitement and expectation started rising in my spirit. When you read these familiar verses, pause and consider why you are drawn or prompted to take this journey. As you wait before the Lord, a longing will begin to well up. That's the Holy Spirit beginning a prayer for you. Write out your prayer to the Father, Jesus, and the Holy Spirit. Here is mine as an example:

> Dear Father God,
>   This is my "in the beginning." In this new venture into Scripture—a new way to connect, communicate, talk, and listen through Your Word—I pray I come to know Your will and how to apply it to my life accurately.
>
> Lord Jesus,
>   You are the Life and Light to me. In the areas of my heart where there is doubt, unbelief, death, and darkness, I pray this journey breaks through and brings life and light into my spirit, my understanding, my walk with You, and my witness of You.

Dear Holy Spirit,

Walk through these Scriptures, chapters, verses, and pages with me. Direct and counsel me, give me wisdom and revelation, disciple me ... that I may reflect my Lord Jesus wherever I go and to whomever I speak.

You know how wonderful small beginnings are! Scripture tells us not to despise them. I often returned to these first pages and sat and shook my head. Only God knew where this winding road would take me or how sweet our conversations would be. *Thank You, Lord Jesus. My heart is full.*

Be mindful of other Scriptures the Holy Spirit may bring to mind. After reading John 1:1–5 and writing my prayer, I immediately thought of:

Jesus: Let the little children come to Me; do not get in their way. For the kingdom of heaven belongs to children like these.

He laid His hands on them, *He prayed with them* (Matthew 19:14–15).

I penned this prayer:

Always and still,
Dearest Jesus,
I am in awe and hold a childlike faith and joy and devotion to You. After 40-plus years, my spirit is childlike still. I do not want life, situations, or circumstances to forbid, restrain, or hinder my coming to You.
Please put Your hands on me and pray ...
Your little sheep,
Mary Jo

I am so glad I paused to listen for the prompting of the Holy Spirit. I had no idea when I wrote out this prayer how God intended to answer it. Weeks later He responded in a most surprising way. But that's for later …

As you write your prayers, trust that the Holy Spirit is helping you pray. Look for and expect answers. But please don't be in a hurry. This journey—*your* journey—is about lingering and listening. Take as much time as you want to meditate on these Scriptures, look up references, or write the verses in your own words. Be as creative as you'd like. Remember, there are no rules.

JOHN 1

Who Am I

In the Gospel of John, the very first words Jesus speaks are recorded in John 1:38:

Jesus: What is it that you want?

The word *want* interested me, so I referenced other translations:

- "What do you seek?" (NASB)
- "What are you looking for?" (ISV)
- "What is it you wish?" (AMPC)

The word *seek* caught my attention. I did some research and found other words to help give definition to my response to Jesus: *looking, searching, desiring.*

I wrote my answer to Jesus' question:

Dearest Lord Jesus,

You have said, "Seek my face." My heart says to you,
"Your face, Lord, do I seek" (Psalm 27:8 ESV).

I desire a safe place to knock, seek, and find You. And there is
no safer place than here.

I am seeking Your voice:

"This is the way; walk in it" (Isaiah 30:21 NIV).

Louder than all the other voices, I seek, desire, need to hear and
know Your voice.

I want to be set, settled, secure in who You are and who I am
   with You.
The disciples were seeking answers, and so am I—answers to
   live by, to build my faith, to give me courage and hope and a
   future.

I lingered here. I looked up the names of Jesus and meditated
on them. I thought of the nature and character of Christ. I
wanted to know, understand, and realize how and who He is
and how He changes me.

It is said we become, reflect, and echo those we spend time
with—those we get to know on an intimate level. I prayed for a
greater awareness and realization of the whole of Christ in my
life and how my life communicates Him to others.

You are
   The Way
   The Truth
   The Life
   I AM the Voice.
   I AM the Door.
   I AM the Bread.
   I AM the Light.
   I AM the Good Shepherd.
   I AM the Son of God.
   I AM the Christ, the Anointed One.
   I AM the Vine.
That is who You are, Lord, and …

I was about to ask, "Who am I?" when He interrupted me
with this Scripture:

"I am the Lord's servant," Mary answered. "May your
word to me be fulfilled" (Luke 1:38 NIV).

That's who I am: the Lord's servant. I'm setting my sights on
    You, Jesus. You alone.
And I am secure in knowing You will
        Speak. Lead. Confirm.
        Protect. Defend. Provide.
            Love, Mary Jo

Well, that was a most enlightening conversation. It was like
lingering over a good cup of tea and talking long enough to get
beyond those "How are you? Fine" questions and answers. Here
at the first, Jesus wanted to establish who He is to me and who I
am to Him.

These are not questions lightly asked or answered. They are
anchors in our walk with God. I remember asking God once,
"How do You see me?" Take time to ask God this question and
hear His heart for you.

Writing down conversations between you and Jesus may
be new to you. Journaling is often a monologue or even a
diary. At times it can be so rigid in the "how" that it stifles
the flow of conversation. Allow God to stretch you in this
area. You won't be sorry. In Jeremiah 30:2, the Lord tells us
to "Write in a book all the words I have spoken to you" (NIV).

Let's keep going. I can hardly wait to share these next verses
with you. Such an invitation!

He Knows My Name

Jesus: Come and see. *Follow Me, and we will camp together*
(John 1:39).

Camping. Such a wilderness, tabernacle, fire of God word!
Everything about this offer excited me. "Come and see" was
clearly a bidding that included an expectation to *see* with my
spiritual eyes what He wanted to show me. I began to pen what
I heard Jesus saying to me:

Dear One,
As we travel together through the Gospel of John,
   Come and see
      Everywhere I went
      Everything I did
         was about *My Father's business.*
   Come and see
      Come with Me
      Let Me show you
         What you need to see, understand, and know to move
         forward.

I felt like one of the disciples who left everything and didn't
return home to pack his bags or say any good-byes. Has God
ever asked you to do something, and you instantly knew you
would? You didn't question, argue the point, or try to reason it
out; you were simply compelled to obey. Jesus is calling us today,
"Come, follow Me," and we have an opportunity to respond.

This is a good time to write down your response to this

personal invitation. Jesus is looking for followers, and you are one He is looking for.

When the Lord calls us, we often have a tendency, like Gideon, to look over our shoulders—"Surely He doesn't mean me?" Jesus was about to tell me just how intentionally, how personally, and how well He knows me by name.

Jesus: Your name is Simon, and your father is called John. But from this day forward you will be known as Peter, the rock (John 1:42).

God wanted to show me how He sees me. He paused to talk about *my name*. As we relate to different people in Scripture, we can see ourselves through the lenses of their experiences and responses to God. Often hidden in their names are keys to what God is calling out in us.

Jesus directed the conversation to my name:

To move forward we need to talk about your name.
Your name is _____.
From this day forward, you will be known as _____.

I listed the names I've been given. I thought of a few biblical men and women I aspire to model my life after. I looked up the meanings of their names. I read their stories and meditated on the characteristics of their lives. I lingered, letting the Holy Spirit speak about the influence of these names on my life.

But it was not enough to ponder what I was aspiring to; it was more important to ask Jesus what *He* was speaking to me in this season.

Lord, what do You see for this season?
What would Your name for me be?

Jesus' disciples did not all look alike. They didn't have identical resumes. What was it about these men, and soon to come women and even children, that elicited a "Follow Me" from Jesus? Was it their pedigree, their influence, their status in the community … or was it their heart? Was this what Jesus saw?

Pause and ask God what name He would speak over you for a season, for a reason, or for a lifetime.

John 1 goes on to relate the wonderful story of Nathanael, who is very surprised by Jesus calling him out in the crowd. Not calling his name but identifying him by his character: *truth-teller.* No guile. No deceit. One who is sincere.

Nathanael (*overhearing Jesus*): How would You know this about me? *We have never met.*

Jesus: *I have been watching you* before Philip invited you here. *Earlier in the day,* you were enjoying *the shade and fruit of* the fig tree. I saw you then (John 1:48).

Bible historians tell us that men would gather in the shade of fig trees to rest, meditate, and ponder the coming Messiah. It makes me smile and respond with a "Yes, God!" He sees me. He knows me. After the hours, weeks, and years of wondering and seeking, I've been found! Nathanael responds with, "You are the One" (John 1:49). His spirit must have felt like yours and mine do when we feel the tug of God on our hearts, and the only possible answer is, *You are the One.*

Jesus then introduces Nathanael to the supernatural that accompanies those who follow Him.

Jesus: Nathanael, if all it takes for you to believe is My telling you I saw you under the fig tree, then what you will see later will astound you. I tell you the truth: *before our journey is complete*, you will see the heavens standing open while heavenly messengers ascend and descend, *swirling* around the Son of Man (John 1:50–51).

Jesus wants to do the same for you and me. There is so much more than we know now or have experienced up to this point. There will always be more. He is so infinite, and He wants *more* for us. Isn't that just like a loving God—wanting more for His children?

Dearest Savior Jesus,
These words are so about this season. I become so ensnared with who I am, where I am, and what I am doing. At times, it's difficult to see clearly. But Your voice says, *Follow Me.*
I tell you the truth, Mary,
Before our journey is complete, you will see the heavens standing open while heavenly messengers ascend and descend swirling around Me and who I am in your midst. You are entering a new season of visitation and habitation, of hearing and knowing My voice, of living supernaturally natural. And it will be My power given to you that will be My gift to you.
You are my gift, Jesus!

Linger over His Word. Listen. Write your response to Jesus' *Follow Me.*

JOHN 2

My Aaron and Hur

John 2 begins with the wedding feast in Cana. Scripture tells us of pending embarrassment for the host due to the wine running out. We read of Mary bringing this situation to our Lord's attention and suggesting Jesus is the answer to the problem.

I had heard this event preached, prayed, and pondered from every possible angle: Mary's position as His mother, Jesus' response, the water pots, the obedience of the servants, the Bride and Groom, the guests ... even the water turning into wine! Every angle. Or so I thought. As I read this story in the light of the personal conversation I was having with Jesus, I saw (or *heard*) new revelation:

Intercession. Standing in the gap. Making an appeal.

God began to shed fresh light on these Scriptures and make them applicable to my current situation.

The story begins with Mary acting as an intercessor and making an appeal on behalf of the host (mediating for him, if you will):

Mary: *The host stands on the brink of embarrassment; there are many guests, and there is no more wine.*

Jesus: Dear woman, is it our problem *they miscalculated when buying wine and inviting guests?* My time has not arrived (John 2:3–4).

Despite His protest, though, Jesus answers the plea (prayer) over and above what was asked, hoped, or dreamed.

> Now to him who is able to do far more abundantly than all that we ask or think (Ephesians 3:20 ESV).

And the outcome is faith.

> When the disciples *and the servants* witnessed this miracle, their faith blossomed (John 2:11).

As He often does when He wants to address something specific in my life, God highlighted a word to begin our conversation: *miscalculated* (v. 4). Jesus asked me to consider two points:

1. I miscalculate and need God to intervene, rescue, or redeem me.
2. Others' miscalculations directly impact me in negative ways.

I'm sure you can relate. How often do we find ourselves in a mess—physically, spiritually, or emotionally? Sometimes it's our own doing. Sometimes it's others' doing. And sometimes it's just plain ugly warfare, whether sickness, death, storms, etc. Like Mary,

- We often find ourselves asking (or imploring) God on behalf of ourselves or others needing God's intervention.
- We know Jesus is the only answer to the problem.
- We pray in faith, and our only counsel (to ourselves or others) is, "Do whatever he tells you" (John 2:5 NIV).

My personal mess had left me at yet another dead end—not just a detour but the very end of my own capacity. I penned this prayer:

Dearest Lord Jesus,
I find myself in a situation/problem/dilemma. I have miscalculated the cost physically, emotionally, and spiritually needed
to accomplish _____. Others have miscalculated the
resources, time, and cost needed to accomplish _____.
I have a problem, and I know You are the only answer.

Then I waited. I lingered. One of the most essential keys to
prayer is *listening*—giving God an opportunity to speak.

Jesus: Fill each water pot with water until it's ready to spill over the
top; then fill a cup, and deliver it (John 2:7–8).

Mary,
I know you are reeling and attempting to regroup physically,
emotionally, and spiritually. There's enough blame to go
around. But this is not about blame. This is about redemption. What I need and want you to do is fill six water pots
with what you have.

So I did. I considered what I had at hand for God to use to
redeem, refocus, and make better than ever before. I pondered
water pots. I identified with them, these earthly vessels made of
clay. I prayed and filled my spiritual vessels of clay with:

1. Worship
2. Faith
3. Word
4. Fear
5. Facts
6. Worry

What are the water pots before you? What would you fill them with? Notice in a few of my water pots, I put struggles as well as strengths. I needed God to take my *worship* and turn it more outward and upward. I needed my *faith* to take every thought captive and break strongholds. I needed more of the *Word* to battle for me and build me up. I needed *fear* to bow to the power of God in my mind and body. I needed *facts* as I see them to be the facts God sees, with tools to walk victoriously. I needed *worry* to turn into a miracle of peace and greater trust in the wisdom and faithfulness of my God.

Weariness had definitely taken up residence in my body and soul, and even hope deferred in my spirit. Jesus said:

Mary,

Are you looking for a sign that breakthrough is coming? Are you needing an external sign to know that you know that you know I am doing an internal work? Are you wanting some reassurance?

> "Wait, my daughter, until you know how the matter turns out; for the man will not rest until he has settled it today" (Ruth 3:18 NASB).

Yes, Lord. You know me so well. I know I'm building spiritual muscles, that in the waiting time I am learning more faith, hope, and love. However, hope deferred does make the heart sick. And I am showing symptoms of being heart-sick. Yes, I would like a sign.

Let's deal with

> Hope postponed grieves the heart;
> but when a dream comes true, life is full *and sweet*
> (Proverbs 13:12).

The dreams you have, especially the ones that seem like they are slipping through your life and fading like a beautiful sunset lost ... the dreams I planted and watered, I will bring to pass. The timing, the how, the what, the who, the when may not be as you have anticipated or expected.

This is where faith takes root.

And patience is planted.

And plans are watered.

And the season will come.

Hindsight will be a great gift for hope deferred. Then, and only then, will you fully see My ways are higher than yours. Your part is to do what you have in your hand today. Is it prayer? Is it praise? Is it pressing in? Is it ...

I don't know.

I do.

Moses's hands grew weary. I gave him an Arron and a Hur. I am sending you your Aaron and Hur too.

Jesus,

Thank You for personally taking time for me. Thank You for caring enough and not playing the guilt or blame game with me. Regardless of whether it was miscalculated or not Your time, You stopped everything. You sat with me. You spoke to me. You gave me strategy to pray, believe, and stand.

And then You took what I had to offer You and changed my heart. You filled my thoughts with Your character, caring, and counsel. And You loved me enough to work all things for the good (Romans 8:28) and for Your glory.

> You sent a heavy downpour *to soak the ground*, O True God. You refreshed the land—*the land* Your people would inherit—when it was *parched and* dry (Psalm 68:9).

And now I can take this new heart, new wine, new understanding, realizing my vessel is full. Now I can take and pour
into a cup and give to others. John 2:11 says, "Their faith
blossomed". Well, so did mine.

> [Jesus] revealed His glory [displaying His deity and His
> great power openly], and His disciples believed [confi-
> dently] in Him [as the Messiah—they adhered to,
> trusted in, and relied on Him] (John 2:11 AMP).

Use my life—any circumstance, situation, or problem that
ONLY You are the answer to …
Be glorified.
Love,
Mary

Over the next days, weeks, and even months, I sought God's
heart about this. Not just about the situation or circumstance
but about my *heart*. About the changes He wanted to make in
me. I knew in my heart:

> I am convinced *and* confident of this very thing, that He
> who has begun a good work in you will [continue to]
> perfect *and* complete it" (Philippians 1:6 AMP).

And I didn't lose sight of the fact that I was just two chapters
away from another water pot encounter with Jesus.

I was quickly discovering this walk through John was more
than just something to do. Jesus was not in a hurry. Just like in
Scripture when He took His time with people and asked His
piercing questions, our journey together was becoming a very
face-to-face, hand-in-hand, real-time encounter.

Dear ones, please take as long as you like. More than that,
though—take as long as Jesus wants to speak to you about the

miracles, changes, and revelations He wants to do in and for your life.

Identify what you need to fill the six water pots in your life with.

What is God working on changing inside you so you can fill up, spill over, and deliver Jesus to others?

oBEy

With the Spirit-inspired, purposeful writing of the Scriptures, we go from the wedding in Cana and the miracle of changing water into wine to lingering in Capernaum with family and friends. John highlights the value and intentionality of our Lord to pull aside, rest, and fellowship. Even with the enormity of establishing His Church, disciplining a team of leaders, and ministering to a growing community of believers, Jesus rested. He sabbath-ed. He retreated to the mountains in the early morning; He escaped to the other side of the lake.

Thank You, Lord, for not just telling us how to live but demonstrating the purposefulness of living life "at the pace and rhythms" God set out for each of us (1 Kings 8:58 MSG).

Mary,

I'm glad you noticed. I was always about My Father's business but only doing what He told Me to do. That requires communication, time, balance, trust, *being*, and not doing. It's what I want the Church to model to the world. Can you do your part? I'll help.

Thank You, Jesus. I'm counting on it. It's not a strong suit of mine. My passion and zeal for the Church and, really, for

You often puts the *doing* part ahead of the *being* part. It's so easy for my passion to get ahead of Your purpose and timing.

Mary,

As we continue our walk through John, remember the spelling test I gave you years ago. How do you spell *obey*? What do the two middle letters spell? oBEy. Obey Me, and you'll learn to BE and not DO. I don't want you to hurry through John. We will linger, laugh, and love along the way. Are you with Me?

Holding tight! I love You!

I love you, too!

Why is Jesus always pointing us to the Father? Because that was His mission. He came to earth to show us the Father, to do the Father's will, and to be the bridge from sin that separated us from God to the promise of eternal life.

Obedience will always be the key to staying focused and aligned. Now is a good time to review areas of your life, especially those regarding being and doing and obeying. Perhaps you will hear, "Well done!" Or perhaps there are areas God wants to bring to light. Whatever the case, take time. Journal your prayers. Write down what God is saying to you.

Effective. Righteous. Prayer.

From lingering in Capernaum to traveling to Jerusalem for Passover, Jesus went to the temple to worship and was met with anything but worship.

I love the sequence of these verses. First, God deals with the issues of my heart, the abiding place for His presence. And then He turns the tables of my heart, my motives, and my wrong thinking over and cleans my house. His priority is always relationship with Him first. After we get this on firm ground, we move to the incident at the temple where Jesus finds His Father's house in great disarray. Things are seriously out of order; man's agenda and selfishness have taken over. What a contrast to the respect for God's house during its construction, when "no hammer, chisel or any other iron tool was heard" out of reverence (1 Kings 6:7 NIV).

Jesus: *What are you still doing here?* Get all your stuff, and haul it out of here! Stop making My Father's house a place for your own profit! (John 2:16).

A prayer rose within me:

From a heart of humility and brokenness,
Lord Jesus,
Raise up a righteous indignation in me and help me pray for
    the Church. Your Bride. Not from a place of judgment or
    criticism but rather from a place of zeal and love and support.
    Oh, Lord, to be that Aaron or Hur supporting our leaders
    and not be numbered with the murmuring and complaining.
    Sanctify my prayers as You have sanctified my heart and
    mind. Oh Lord, I want You to be proud of Your Church;
    after all, we carry Your name. We serve in Your name. We
    love in Your name. Help me, Lord.

Prayer.
Effective. Righteous. Prayer.
Honestly, I get frustrated. I get disheartened with delay. I get heartbroken when prayer doesn't seem like I'm doing enough.

God interrupted my thoughts:

Why do you minimize the
>value,
>>victories,
>>>the beyond the veil
>>of your prayer life,
>As if you had something to do with it?
I planted.
>I watered.
>>I harvested your prayer life.
Why do you treat what is holy as if it is unholy?
Oh, Lord Jesus,
You are right to bring correction. I am so sorry. Please forgive
>me. I didn't see it this way. I know it's the most wonderful
>gift You have done for me. You created me to pray. You
>opened Your arms, heart, will, Word, and works through
>this gift of prayer. It is a treasured, eternal gift, and I will
>treat it as holy ... Amen.
Mary,
I am putting My Spirit in you to discern how to pray. As I wept
>over the city, you shall weep over the Church. As a mother
>cries for her unborn child, you shall groan for the unborn
>promises of My church yet to be birthed. Always remember
>I did not come to destroy a building. I came to cleanse hearts
>and motives and restore purity and humility and holiness. I
>will always be about people.
I will give you signs (John 2:19) to direct your prayers. Watch.
>See. Pray. I am the Temple rebuilt after three days, and I am
>still at work with the Father and the Holy Spirit to tear down
>the works of the enemy and build up My Bride, the Church.

Amen!
Amen!
So be it!
So be it!

Whew! That conversation was powerful. It could fill a library of books. Prayer is such a powerful word that encompasses the whole of our relationship and partnership with God. It's the greatest gift—a two-way conversation that will take me from here to eternity. And God has everything to do with it.

Prayer is being and doing.
Prayer is relationship and partnership.
Prayer is the earthly echo of God's heart.
Prayer is representing God on earth.
Prayer is connecting heaven to earth.
Prayer is intimate.
Prayer is Scripture-breathed.
Prayer is powerful.
Prayer is easy.
Prayer is hard work.

My list of what prayer is could go on and on. I believe we *live* prayer; it is not just what we do but *who* we are.

Your prayer life—your prayer DNA—is uniquely yours. It's a facet of God expressed as only you can. And God's reply is His personal expression of love for you. What an honor. What joy! Jesus wants to reveal Himself to you through your prayers. Will you let Him?

JOHN 3

My "Born Again"

In the quiet of the night, Nicodemus slips away from the "some of us [who] have been talking" (John 3:2) to seek some real answers. That's so often what my time with God is about—seeking answers. We all have unanswered questions, most of all about God, eternity, and the things that make sense of this earthly life. And the very first thing Jesus has to say is the most profound, summarize-the-whole-of-Scripture-into-one-verse sentence, like only He can do.

Jesus: I tell you the truth: only someone who experiences birth for a second time can *hope to* see the kingdom of God (John 3:3).

If there ever was a chapter to camp out in, this is it. Here is Nicodemus, who by his beliefs, is already *born again*—a term very familiar to him. According to Pharisaic Judaism, there were multiple ways to be *born again*, including:

- Bar mitzvah
- Marriage
- Rabbinic ordination
- Become the head of a rabbinical school

Nicodemus had done all four![1] In the context of his traditional beliefs, his question to Jesus makes perfect sense: "How can an

---

[1] Rabbi Barry Rubin, ed., *The Complete Jewish Study Bible: Illuminating the Jewishness of God's Word* (Peabody, MA: Hendrickson Publishers, 2016), 1525.

old man go back into his mother's womb and be born again?" (John 3:4 NLT)

Jesus: I tell you the truth, if someone does not experience water and Spirit birth, there's no chance he will make it into God's kingdom (John 3:5).

Isn't that just like Jesus—to speak to the core, to the truth of what we thought we were asking?

We all have our own stories, each of us drawn by the Spirit in a unique way to the same place of understanding: *God loves me. The Father sent Jesus to earth to save me from sin and to restore my relationship with Him. Now we are united in heart, and we will spend eternity together.*

What a time to pause and ponder and reflect.

Or …

What a time to respond to the Holy Spirit.

> God, I know I have not lived my life for You. I know I sin, and my sin separates me from You. I believe Jesus is God and came to earth for me. I ask You to forgive me of all my sins. Help me begin to live as a follower of my Lord and Savior, Jesus. Thank You for the promise of the Holy Spirit who will lead me, teach me, and counsel me as I follow You. From now until eternity. Amen.

Lord Jesus,

At the tender age of 29, I remember the moment when years of religion were erased, and I was invited into a relationship with You. I recall the minute my spirit spoke to my mind, and I understood for the first time what Scriptures meant about

a life surrendered to God,

a life committed to following You,

a life that had come to an end here on earth to be
born again for eternity.

Isn't your personal story your favorite? Your journey from
darkness to light. Your testimony. Your "born again." It bears
writing down. Jesus may even want to add to your insight, your
point of decision, your before and after. Relish these memories
and dream about the days to come.

Favor

Mary
Born "anew" you were
those many years ago.
Your faith, hope, and love in Me
caused those seeds to grow.
You've been an oak, a fig,
an olive tree—three.
I've planted, and you've watered
so others would see Me.
This season, this new thing
I'm doing for you:
it's about the Tree of Life
and the fruit I'll produce too!

I lingered here. For weeks I pondered and prayed about this
new season. I referenced *new* in the Scriptures:

- new cart (1 Chronicles 13:7)
- new song (Psalm 33:3)

- new threshing instrument (Isaiah 41:15)
- new thing springing forth (Isaiah 43:19).

Dear Lord Jesus,

How aware I am of how aware You are of where I've been, where I am, and where You are taking me. Following You has always involved living outside my comfort zone, often walking in faith to that still, small voice of the Holy Spirit. If I had a choice it would be for trumpets to blow and angels to herald, *"This is the way; walk in it!"* But this I know: You have always gone before me and prepared the way. You give favor with You and others.

> "For he who finds me finds life
> And obtains favor from the Lord"
> (Proverbs 8:35 NASB).

A favorite quote by Lance Wallnau on *favor* has always encouraged and strengthened me when I walk into the unknown following You:

> Favor is the affection of God toward you that releases an influence through you so that other people are inclined to like, trust and cooperate with you.[2]

That alone, God—that You have affection toward me—makes any unknown worth it. It is so humbling and blesses me beyond what I can say.

I pray now for peace and patience as I wait on You. I ask for and thank You for favor with You and man as I move forward trusting and obeying.

Love, Mary

---

[2] Lance Wallnau, "The Force Of Favor," Identity Network Christian Resources, accessed March 12, 2018, http://www.identitynetwork.net/apps/articles/default.asp?articleid=29647.

Favor is not something you can learn, borrow, or buy. Favor is the result, the fruit, the overflow of Christ in me, the hope of glory. Cultivating the presence of God; spending time in personal worship; meditating on the Word, obeying His voice; praying; interceding; crying out to God … The overflow is favor. It's not the goal. *It's the gift: His presence.*

This speaks so well to the position we have in Christ. Time and time again, I see how God does so much with my so little. I am in awe of the honor of carrying God's presence and how hosting it produces such favor with Him and others in my life.

What does favor look like in your life? Do a Scripture study on this word. Listen to Lance Wallnau's teachings on favor. Read Dutch Sheets' book *The Pleasure of His Company*. Pursue God's presence and watch His goodness, mercy, and favor follow. It is the manifestation of His affection toward you.

By now, your journal pages are filling up with God-triggered conversations. I pray that prayer is taking on a whole new dimension of relationship for you. Keep journaling. God has more to say!

Legacy

Jesus and I had many long conversations traveling through Scripture. We talked about prayer and intercession; I was created to pray. We talked about numbering my days; none of us is guaranteed tomorrow. I read Ecclesiastes. We talked at length about life and the things that matter to Him and, therefore, matter to me. God was renewing my mind and heart and adding value to the days at hand.

What did He want this new season to look like? What does legacy mean to Him?

> The true legacy of a servant will not be determined by what he has done but by what others do as a result of what he has done.
>
> —Wayne Cordeiro[3]

This quote spoke volumes to me. What seeds am I planting—in prayer and intercession, in living and loving, in mentoring and modeling following Jesus—that will be lived out long after I am forgotten? *Legacy.*

Mary,

As you pray and ponder legacy, remember this:

　My legacy is people.

　I came to earth for one reason: people.

> Because the Light, *sent from God*, pierced through the world's darkness (John 3:19).

Lord Jesus,

This so reminds me of Genesis 1—the Light penetrated

　the darkness. That moment You pierced my heart,

　March 16, 1976; when my heart,

　seeking,

　　surrendered,

　　　and the Spirit took up residence.

From day one, Daughter, I wanted you to "comprehend *the necessity of life in the Spirit*" (John 3:10).

I have never known another way!

---

[3] Wayne Cordeiro, *The Dream Releasers: How to Help Others Realize Their Dreams While Achieving Your Own* (Ventura: Regal, 2002).

Mary,
Speak about what you know. Give evidence to what you have
seen. Give words to your earthly realities from the perspec-
tive of your heavenly realities.
You mean like, "On earth as *it is* in heaven" (Matthew 6:10 NKJV).
Lord Jesus, You were heaven on earth. You are now the
earthly reality that sheds light and revelation through the
Spirit about the reality of heaven.
You are the Word.
   You are the Light.
      You are God made man.
         You literally brought heaven to earth.
Help me "see" You.
Mary, speak about what you know. Give evidence to what you see.
You, Jesus, are the evidence.
Help me give voice to what I know.

> Those who *abandon deceit* and embrace what is true, they
> will enter into the light where it will be clear that all their
> deeds come from God (John 3:21).

You, Lord Jesus, are the Light of the World.
   You are the Word, and Your Word lights my path.
      Keep me, Lord. Keep me following You.

You are never too young to consider your legacy. And you are
never too old to ponder what it is you are leaving for others to
run this race with Christ. What is your spiritual will? What is it
you want God to continue to breathe His Spirit on after you are
gone? Your heart-print. Your prayers. Your love. Your forgiveness. Your kindness. Your mercy.
   Talk to Jesus about this. After all, you are His legacy.

My Re-Baptism

As I turned the page of my Bible toward the next red-letter words, I paused on the Scriptures relating John and Jesus' disciples. As an infant, my parents had me baptized by sprinkling. As a young adult, following a personal surrender of my life to God and reading Scriptures on the outward expression of faith in Christ, I was immersed in water baptism. Years later, after wrestling with depression, I found myself sitting in a church baptism service. God had pulled me out of my miry pit, and I had landed firm in my faith and who I was in Christ. I was set free! Dressed in my Sunday best and celebrating the full truth of going down into the waters dead in sin and rising to my new life in Christ, I ran to the front and participated in a spirit-and-truth baptism. That was June 2, 1991.

The following morning, I picked up a flip calendar I kept next to my prayer chair. It said:

> One cannot step twice in the same river, for fresh waters are forever flowing around us.
>
> —Heraclitus

> Father, keep me from the futile thoughts of constantly reliving past experiences. Help me to glean your benefits from the past and to move forward with confidence. Amen.[4]

I paused to give thanks to God, "for my heart is set on a pilgrimage" (Psalm 84:5), and He sealed the past season with the fresh waters of baptism and revelation. He set me free in Christ to be and do all He planned and purposed for me.

---

[4] Mary Bevis and Jeneanne Sieck, "June 2" in *Bless Your Heart: Each New Day* (Heartland Samplers, 1987).

JOHN 4

The Well

If there is one thing I learned from this red-letter journey, it is that Jesus was *never* in a hurry. Scripture says He needed to go to Samaria; He had a divine appointment with the woman at the well. Jesus also had a divine appointment with me, but I had to slow down, take a deep breath, and prepare to drink some deep well-water. I recorded our first conversation about John 4 in December, and two months later, I found myself asking God, "Do You realize we are *still* at the well?" (It wouldn't be until April that we moved on to chapter 5.)

Jesus was in no hurry to get me through John 4. He lingered. We talked. I wrestled with some situations in my life. I prayed about the things that concerned me, searching the Scriptures for what God had to say. And He certainly did have something to say. There were some nonnegotiable, spirit and truth revelations He really needed and wanted me to grasp.

I was in a time of transition. (Actually, I've learned we are always "transitioning": continuously changing from glory to glory and moving forward in His plans and purposes.) In this particular season, I was really counting my days—*Lord, what do You want this to look like?*

Do you have something weighing on your spirit today? Do you have questions needing answers? Have you found yourself wrapped in what feels more like a coat of religion than a mantle of relationship? Now is the time to lay aside preconceived ideas about conversations with God and simply ask Jesus to speak truth to you. He is ready to meet you right where you are.

Welcome to the well.

Give Me a Drink

It was another ordinary, things on my mind, cares and concerns kind of day. Swirling around in my heart was a dust storm of medical reports, projects, plans, dreams, ideas, deadlines, and so much more. Barely settled into my prayer chair, I began wondering where to start this conversation. I had a real "all who are weary and heavy-laden"[1] moment.

Then I remembered: "I'm going somewhere special today! I have a divine appointment already scheduled. I have Someone who has intentionally gone out of His way to meet with me. I'm going to the well. Not just any well. I'm going to the *John 4 well.*" And just like that, my spirit sensed an "I will give you rest"[2] relief.

Drawn to the well,
    Thinking it was just another day.
Drawn to the well,
    My lot in life—this is just the way.
Drawn to the well,
    A stranger sitting there.

Jesus: Would you *draw water, and* give Me a drink? (John 4:8).

Of course, Lord. I would do whatever You ask.
    But ...

---

[1] Matthew 11:28a NASB.
[2] Matthew 11:28b NASB.

living water
fountain of life

the Jesus

Well

need to go through Samaria

I needed it more!

RELIGION TO RELATIONSHIP

SPIRIT & truth

WELL DONE

Redig promises
Open dry wells
Dig new wells

Linger at the Well
of the One who
sees me
the living One

Rest

Anchors my prayer life

Sabbath

Anchors my

Rest

War · Wrestle · Contend · from a place of rest

" Our God and God of our Father,
be pleased with our rest."

JEWISH SABBATH AMIDAH

JOHN 4 | 31

My bucket has run dry. It is empty.

How could this be? Just months ago, there was a prophetic word:

> I see a spilling over you, a spilling out—this well that never seems to run dry. This overflow spilling out of your heart is going to get everyone here wet....

Let Me tell you
  how this could happen.
Let Me tell you
  how to fill it up again.
Let Me tell you how the
  well will spill over.
Then, when I say to you, "Would you draw water and give Me a
  drink?", you will no longer question how.

A great battle waged in my mind. I was in the middle of a *lay it all down* season—a hands-off, I've got this, do you trust Me, I desire obedience rather than sacrifice kind of season. But in the middle of all the noise in my head, I began to sense a gentle whisper and waves of grace as beloved Scriptures interrupted my thoughts.

> "[Hush!] Be silent before the Lord God"
> (Zephaniah 1:7 AMP).

> "Sit still, my daughter, until you know how the matter
> will turn out; for the man will not rest until he has
> concluded the matter this day" (Ruth 3:18 NKJV).

Daughter,
Dear One,
  Mary,
You've come to the well this season,

this pause,
this holy hush.
You've come to the well with the same pattern of drawing,
same mindset,
same strongholds.
But you don't know the gift of God or who is asking you for a
drink.
If
you
did ...
You would ask for something greater.
Indeed, your well has run dry.
There is nothing to draw from.
My desire is to tap into the wellspring within you
that will give you life from here to eternity.
You will never be thirsty again.
Lord Jesus,
This is what I'm asking. I don't want to keep going around the
same mountain.
I want to tap into the wellspring,
the revelation,
the how of the "who,"
and move forward in loving,
living,
and serving You.
You said if I draw from You, the Living Water, then I will never
thirst again. Then, I'm missing something. My well runs
dry. The woman at the well's response to Your question
or directive was from her tree of knowledge, much like
Nicodemus, and not from the Tree of Life where the real
living water comes from.

You discern correctly, Mary.

My Dearest Lord Jesus,

I have loved stepping into Scripture and talking with You.

This season, can You help me find the pieces of my heart I have lost?

Holy Spirit, breathe life over those places that were joyful, life-giving,

God-pleasing places.

Those places that cause others to seek You,

draw near to You,

want to know You.

That place of peace,

The unforced rhythm of grace place,

That place of sweet communion.

How, Lord Jesus, do I find my way back?

Devoted Daughter,

Mary

Dear One,

You ask how—

Hold fast.

Don't hold on too tightly.

Hold what I put in your hands;

Let go of the rest.

Let go of

- Assumption
- Presumption
- Your expectations
- Others' expectations
- The past
- The future

I was prompted to search the Scriptures for "hold fast," and I was captured by what God was saying to me.

> My uprightness *and* my right standing with God I hold fast and will not let them go; my heart does not reproach me for any of my days *and* it shall not reproach me as long as I live (Job 27:6 AMPC).

> "Let your heart hold fast my words;
>   Keep my commandments and live" (Proverbs 4:4 AMP).

> Hold fast the pattern of sound words which you have heard from me, in faith and love which are in Christ Jesus (2 Timothy 1:13 NKJV).

> Holding fast the word of life, so that I may rejoice in the day of Christ that I have not run in vain or labored in vain (Philippians 2:16 NKJV).

> Let us hold fast the confession of *our* hope without wavering, for He who promised *is* faithful (Hebrews 10:23 NKJV).

I will never, ever—from now until eternity—get over how God can speak a word or phrase, give a picture, or drop a Scripture into the conversation and give depth, life, hope, faith, and love. How does He do that time and time again? Our God is alive, and He lives in us!

> Thank You, Jesus, for coming and showing us the way. For being the Word—active and alive, sharper than a two-edged sword. For giving hope to the hopeless. For being the anchor of our faith and bringing love and life to every place the enemy tries to bring death and destruction.

Begin the conversation with Jesus that will take you from religion to relationship, from questions to answers, from dogma to revelation. The Lord knows all about you—where you've been, what you've done, and all your strengths and weaknesses. Today, He asks you for a drink of water. What will you say?

Linger

My days turned into weeks as I continued to return to the well. I spent time pondering and activating these verses in my thoughts, words, and actions. I searched the Scriptures when prompted with a word, picture, or thought. I continued to press into Jesus as I was drawn to the well by the Holy Spirit.

Lord,
There is an increased knowing and confidence and conviction
  that I cannot move forward without You. I'm still at the
  well. I am not ready to "run to the town people and tell them
  about You."
Daughter,
  Sit.
    Sit still.
  Sit at the well.
There is more we need—and I want—to talk about. My desire
  is your increased knowing, confidence, and conviction that
  is birthed in 2 Chronicles 12:8—"long for *the ease of* serving
  Me":
  • ease
  • unforced rhythms of grace
  • rest in well-doing
  • equally yoked to you
  • righteous burdens

It's not so much about the location of the well,
    nor about what's in your hand.
It's about the source of where,
    the focus of who,
    the reason of why.
I am the Where,
    the Who,
      the Why.
Our *unexpectantly* is
    not an encounter,
      not an exchange;
rather, an eclipse.
Mary,
    This eclipse is the *something greater,*
    the living water (John 4:10).
You heard Me well just now. I whispered, "You must decrease
    as I increase." This season ahead will be marked by this
    encounter, exchange, and eclipse at the well.
Settle in on Who you know.

Jesus: The Anointed is speaking to you. I am the One you have been
    looking for (John 4:26).

I meditated on the names of God and studied the character of Father, Son, and Holy Spirit. Friends, I love the Trinity relationship God is working out in us. This is a true picture of prayer in action!

- The Father wants to have direct communion with us, so He sent the Son to redeem us.
- The Son (Jesus) died, rose again, and gave us the Holy Spirit.

- The Holy Spirit intercedes for us and draws our hearts to the Son, who always points us back to the Father.

This ongoing, three-cord strong relationship will impact every area of your life—your prayers, your heart, and your home.

Lord Jesus,
For the things You want to show me, to say, to settle—I surrender all.
Jesus, may I ask one thing?
Yes, Daughter. Ask for the greater things.
In these last years, in this precious time I have left and the plans You have for me, the prayers You put in me, the purposes You created me for ...
I'll want to finish. To complete all You desired for me to do.
To me, this is the "greater" (not *my* will, dreams, or desires).
Mary,
My life on this earth was so much more about who I *am* versus what I did. BE first. Do second. oBEy.

What is your greater thing? What is your deepest eternal desire? Jesus wants to talk to you about it. He has a plan. A purpose. A process. He will take you from where you are to where He wants you to *be*.
Ask. Listen. Journal.
God has a plan.
I have a prayer.
God has a purpose.
I have a prayer.
God has a process.
I have a prayer.

It takes time to absorb truth and revelation. It takes meditating, marinating, and decision-making. It takes the Holy Spirit. There are no microwave relationships with Jesus. Just eternal ones.

Hand in Hand

I began this journey because I wanted to know my Savior better—to walk closer with Him and become more discipled in His ways. One particular day, though, I found myself needing a Friend. One who would stick closer than a brother. One who knew me better than I knew myself and believed more for me than I ever could.

I wrote:

Jesus, Friend,
  Although that (friend) is not until chapter 16, today I need a friend.
  I remember You said to hold fast but don't hold on to …

Then Jesus interrupted me:

Give Me your hand.

"Literally?" I asked. I stopped, and for some Spirit-led reason, I laid my right hand on the left side of the journal and turned it palm up. I traced my hand, opened upward for the Lord to fill.

This bothered me, though. Why in the world would I use my right hand on the left side of the paper? To fix this, I laid my left hand, palm up, on the right side of the journal and traced it as well. I wanted to show willingness, but there was more ...

The reason the Spirit had me trace my hands this way would become apparent later, but at that moment, I found the answer to "I need a friend." It was Jesus, walking hand in hand with me. I paused and recalled that on the first page of my journal I had talked to the Lord about His hands! (This is the beauty of walking into the Scriptures with Jesus—finding exactly what I need for today and also discovering further depth and meaning as the journey continues.)

Although I was only a few chapters into John, Jesus had already shown me so much about who He is and what He wants for me. My heart yearned to begin living from the *being* with Jesus that overflows to the *doing* with Him. I thought of what this must have been like for this woman at the well, the one we have heard so much about.

Unsettled.

Untethered.

Uncertain.

I wrote about "carpet time" in my first book, *Adventures in Prayer: A 40-Day Journey.* I recalled the times I would lay prostrate before the Lord. My prayers were wordless, but my heart was crying out for more of Him. I would lay submitted to the ministry of the Holy Spirit, trusting there would be more of God and less of me when I stood up.

This was another such moment. Wordless. Just knowing I needed more of Him. I lay before the Lord, wondering about this journey to date. This lingering at the well. What He was doing in me that I wasn't fully aware of.

When I returned to my prayer chair, I wrote:

"Martha" came to the well
    She left "Mary."
"Martha" had five husbands
    She left a Bride.
"Martha" carried a water pot
    She left empty-handed
for
    She had more than a water pot could hold.
The enemy who seeks to steal, kill, and destroy is putting up a
    good fight.
    Harassed
    Hindered
    Hassled
    Mary,
    You have
    lost sight and it
    hurts.
    I have
    not lost sight,
    and
    I heal hurts.
    Stay at the well.

Jesus: I have food to eat that you know nothing about (John 4:32).

One aspect of this journey that particularly blessed me was how often related Scriptures cropped up in my prayers. Jesus kept weaving verses in and out of our conversations.

Set. Settled. Secure.
Jesus, it's a good thing we've paused at the well. I know I can be
    renewed and refreshed and reset at this place.

The well:
   my place to meet,
   our Tent of Meeting,
   our origination,
   destination,
   default,
   place to be.

He Sees Me

I awoke especially early one day, in time to watch the sunrise. Every time I see the gorgeous, God-painted sky, I lament having missed so many. I promise myself I am going to change my ways and become an early to bed, early to rise person. (Easier said than done, though.) That morning, I climbed the stairs to my prayer room with a spirit of anticipation.

I hope that's how you come to prayer. Anticipating. Expectant. Hopeful. I hope you have your journal in your hand and your Bible on your lap. Let's get started.

Next to my prayer chair is a stack of devotionals. Often, my eyes will wander and land on a certain one. And so the adventure begins. That particular morning, I picked up *A Hebrew Word for the Day* and randomly opened to December 29:

> **Beerlahairoi:** "The Well of the Living One Who Sees Me" … a symbol of life and value[3]

Oh, this was going to be good! I looked up *Beerlahairoi* online and found:

---

[3] J.D. Watson, *A Hebrew Word for the Day: Key Words from the Old Testament* (Chattanooga, TN: AMG Reference, 2010), 364.

"The well of him that liveth and seeth me," or, as some render it, "the well of the vision of life," the well where the Lord met with Hagar (Genesis 16:7–14). Isaac dwelt beside this well (24:62; 25:11).[4]

My heart started to race. God had been waiting for me to wake up so we could talk more about what the well means.

I know.
I know.
I know.
You have something to say.
We've lingered at the well.
I feel so badly that it got so bad, so worn out. I feel like I could have prevented this if I had been more disciplined, more discerning, more discreet.
There is more going on than you knew.
There is more going on than you see.
I AM the Living One who sees you.

Sometimes I don't know how to handle the closeness of God, the nearness of His voice, or the reality of connecting me with GOD! It seems so surreal—the God of the universe showing up in my prayer room just like Jesus showed up at the well. Sometimes I have to just sit and hug my Bible as my heart fills with wonder and awe.

A song by Misty Edwards came to my mind at that moment: "I Knew What I Was Getting Into."[5] God began speaking to

4 "Beer-Lahai-Roi Definition and Meaning - Bible Dictionary." 2018. Bible Study Tools, accessed March 21, 2018, https://www.biblestudytools.com/dictionary/beer-lahai-roi/.

5 Misty Edwards, "I Knew What I Was Getting Into," in *Joy*, Forerunner Music, 2014, CD.

me through the lyrics, which declare that He chose me—on purpose! He has full knowledge of all my quirks, my past mistakes, and my future failures. He knows me better than I know myself. Yet He has never had even the slightest second thought about saying, "Mary, you are Mine!" When I can't see past my mess, He can. And He does. He sees the future victories and joy, even when all I see is the present defeat and misery.

I needed to hear this. I needed to let this song wash over me. I needed a good cry. I had just gone through a very difficult and heartbreaking personal setback. I was misunderstood. Accused. Betrayed. My public persona was "steady as she goes," but my private life was devastated. This is who Jesus met with that morning.

I feel so uncovered, so disconnected, so vulnerable.
I needed You.
　　I was there.
　　I am here.
I can and want to fight the good fight.
I don't want to give up, give in, quit.
But my body, my emotions, my mind … frazzled and frayed.
　　I'm about to teach you, Daughter, how you will move
　　forward and finish well. Listen closely.

I had a choice: come to my own defense or allow God to take the fragmented pieces of destiny and dreams, promises and plans, and put them back together again. I chose the latter.

God met me in my hour of need. He will meet you, too. How will He speak to you? In the exact way you need. For me on that day, it was a song, a Scripture, and a picture. These became the rope I hung onto that kept me from free falling.

When I wrote my prayer out, the word "frayed" caught my attention. I did a Scripture word search and found this reference in Exodus 28:32: "That it will not tear *or fray*" (AMP). This verse refers to the High Priest's robe, which was required to have a hem around the edge of the opening to prevent fraying.

Jesus, so much!

The robe was for the High Priest, one worthy to stand before the Lord. I believe this is one thing You want to do at the well, and it will prepare me for the days ahead. To pray. To intercede. To stand in the gap. To worship. To connect heaven to earth. To connect You to others and others to You. Whatever You want to do in my body, soul, spirit … do it, Lord. I surrender all. Hem me in, Lord, so I will not fray or frazzle. Strengthen the binding around my prayer life that I may finish well.

Dear One,

I'm about to redraw the boundary lines around you. You will be hemmed in. I am binding the woven work of My plans for you, and it will not fray.

I have declared, "Enough is Enough!"

Let heaven and earth and every strategy of the enemy take notice.

Enough is enough!

What is bound in heaven is bound on earth.

What is loosed in heaven is loosed on earth.

You will see the binding and the loosing of My plans and purposes for this season, My reason, and your lifetime.

You have loved Me well.

You will now begin to serve Me at the well, from the well.

_____ will come to you.
You will have water for them to draw from.
    Hear Me on this, _____: you are _____, and
    you will never run dry again.
So be it.
    Let it be done according to Your will.
    Nothing is impossible with You.
    You are the Master Weaver.

Dear friends, this declaration from Jesus has several blanks. These are intentional. I want you to pray and fill them in. Allow God to speak to you about what He is doing in your life and why. My desire is for you to hear God say, "Enough is enough!" over the battles you are waging. I have the advantage of writing this book years after I did this journey. I have the gift of hindsight to see how God faithfully did what He said He was going to do.

Keep pondering,
    Sweet Mary.
Keep digging this well,
    Dear One.
Keep resting and remembering
    I am at work.
Lord Jesus,
The Word is so rich in truth and life and confidence and love.
Forgive me for the years I grazed Your Word instead of sitting
    for an entire meal.
It's time for questions and answers. I want to leave this season at
    the well with clarity
                courage
                conviction

to move forward in be-ing and do-ing what
You have planned for me.
"Follow Me,"
You say.
Follow You
every day.
"Follow Me"—
My heart's desire.
Follow You,
hemmed in by Your fire.

Mary,
You are having a personal revival of fire. Your prayer is an exact
echo of My will for you.

"For I," declares the Lord, "will be a wall of fire around her,
and I will be the glory in her midst" (Zechariah 2:5 NASB).

I prepared to leave my prayer room, a quiet confidence
beginning to take root. There was more than a settling in my
spirit; there was a song in my heart. I was leaving hand in hand
with Jesus—the One who tells my wind and waves, "Be still!"

My Well

Days. Weeks. Months. Still at the well. This is not to say
I didn't spent time with Jesus elsewhere. I had regular study
times and reading times, and I journaled other aspects of what
God was saying and doing in my life. There was prayer and
fasting and feasting (holidays), all time spent with the Lord.
But this red-letter journal was set apart. It was used solely for
walking hand in hand with Jesus through the Gospel of John.

No longer was I in a hurry. This was not a 21-day project to be finished in time for Christmas and the New Year's fast. No, this journey required lingering. Meditating. Working out what Jesus was saying to me. Obeying and believing the work He was doing inside me.

I sensed we were nearing the time to move on from John 4. Part of me didn't want to. I felt a bit like Peter at the transfiguration: "Lord, couldn't I just build a tent here for You and me?" But there were places to go and things to do. More Scripture conversations. More revelations. More *getting to know my Jesus*.

Dear One,
   I need you to know
   You have followed in My footprints
      and blazed a trail.
   Now, we will walk hand in hand ,
   and that will make all the difference.

      Do two people walk hand in hand
         if they aren't going to the same place?
         (Amos 3:3 MSG).

So, Daughter,
   My hands resting on yours,
   Our hands clasped in partnership …
   You won't lose the way.
You need to know I was there
   From the moment truth found its way into your heart.
But that was not the beginning.
Before,
   Before "in the beginning,"
      I was there,
         and so were you.

You have to, need to, I so want you to know
  you were there.
Spirit Truth.
  Say goodbye to any form of religion.
  Say yes to relationship.
  This, Dear One, as we prepare to leave the well.
Prepared, Lord, for You and the Holy Spirit to walk me
  through areas in my heart and soul and mind that hindered,
  harassed, and held me from rest.
We lingered at the well of real, authentic worship in spirit and
  truth.
The well of "Living One who sees me."
Your well is
  shallow
    to deep.
Some who will come to your well will quickly get a drink and go
  their way.
Some will come to linger and draw from the deepest part.
        Splashing.
      Sipping.
    Soaking.
I know you've enjoyed this linger, Dear One.
  It's been a long journey to get here.
    But I've been waiting.
Now, Dear One,
It's time to leave the well.
However, we will return here now and again.
Dear Lord Jesus,
  If this was all, it would be more than enough.
  I'm feeling very
    set,

settled,

secure

at the well.

But like the woman at the well, there are places to go and people to tell.

Savior. Redeemer. Shepherd.

Lead the way. I will follow.

Mary,

When she left the well, she had a

marriage,

miracle,

message.

All from a moment, and so will you.

Mary, remember the well.

My Lord,

How could I forget?

But I sense a commandment, not a request.

This meeting was too important not to remember.

I will

remember the well.

I begin renewed, redeemed, revived. Ready to "begin my faith journey" (John 4:42).

Love, Your Mary

Friends, the well left a fragrance that permeated the remainder of my walking and talking with Jesus through the book of John. It taught me the value of lingering. The importance of listening. The gift of being loved and loving in return.

I learned some lifelong prayer lessons. This encounter with my Lord, my Savior, at the well eclipsed what I had known or believed about our relationship up to that point. It certainly had nothing to do with religion. It had everything to do with Jesus: God, Human, Teacher, Lord, and Friend.

I hope you'll stay as long as you need to. As long as He needs you to. There is an anointing on this time, a Spirit-filled blessing that awaits you. Don't miss out. Keep journaling. And when you are ready, I'll be waiting.

It Is Well

On the way to John 5, Jesus has a brief but life-changing conversation with a government official. This man was desperate for Jesus to heal his near-death son. Without Jesus, there was no hope. In so many ways this describes how I come to the Lord in prayer: desperate, fearful, hopeless. In the middle of this father's imploring, though, I found a key to prayer. John 4:49 says: "**Jesus** (*interrupting him*) …".

"Interrupting him." Lord, please interrupt my prayer conversation with You anytime.

How many times have I run ahead of God with potential answers, possible solutions, and promising ideas? What if, instead, I sit, wait, and be still? What if I quiet myself before my God and allow Him to interrupt me?

> When he heard the voice of Jesus, faith took hold of him (John 4:50).

The peace that quiets storms, the presence that calms fears, and the power that releases faith is ready and waiting. Dear friends, allow God to interrupt your prayers. Let faith take hold.

JOHN 5

Line in the Sand

There are times in our walk with Jesus that are so life-altering and mind-changing that they draw an invisible line in the invisible sand of our existence. This red-letter journey was certainly one of those times, and if my line could speak, it would say, "Here, Mary Jo crossed over to a new way of breathing in the Word of God and praying."

The Holy Spirit pressed pause on all my busyness and interrupted my long list with His one Word. He introduced me to a pace and rhythm of relationship with Jesus. I wonder if this is what it felt like to be Enoch.

Before the written Scriptures, prayer gatherings, prayer partners, and prayer groups … Before books and seminars and conferences on how to pray … Before preaching, teaching, and blogging … Before all these things, there was communion between God and a man named Enoch. Enoch lived in habitual fellowship with the Lord, so much so that the Bible remembers him this way:

> Enoch lived a total of 365 years, communing with God—and then he was there no longer, because God had taken him (Genesis 5:23–24 isv).

Enoch *lived* prayer. God revealed Himself to Enoch, and He desires to do the same for you and me. The Holy Spirit draws us, teaches us, instructs us, directs us, and counsels us. And the same Holy Spirit who developed a prayer life in Enoch is available to every believer.

Enoch's name means "dedicated and disciplined." This is the key to connecting with God the way Enoch did. *Dedicate* yourself to the pursuit of God. Devote yourself to seeking Him—in the good times, the bad times, the meantime, all the time. Pursue God! What a heavenly ambition to have. Getting to know the One who created you and for whom you were created. Oh, the things He has to say. Oh, the things He wants to do!

It takes *discipline*. Allow the Holy Spirit to hem you in. When the eyes of your heart begin to wander, quickly return them to the only true Source of life.

> Oh, how I love Your law!
>   I fix my mind on it all day long.
> Your commands make me wiser than my enemies
>   Because they are always with me
>   (Psalm 119:97–98).

Ask the Holy Spirit to give you doable, practical steps to learn and grow in communion with God. Remove the walls, religious boxes, and restrictions you may put on your prayer life.

You listen. He'll talk. You talk. He'll listen.

Living prayer is a life hemmed in by devotional time, Scripture reading, meditating, and other prayer disciplines. But at the heart of prayer is *communion*—walking and talking with God. It is connecting your mind, heart, and spirit to Him. Just as you might walk and talk with a loved one, sharing the events of the day and talking about hopes, dreams, and disappointments, God created you to share this intimacy with Him.

"There no longer" like Enoch—my line in the sand. Now it's time to walk into John 5.

So Many Questions

Good morning, Lord Jesus.

I love early mornings before the first sliver of light breaks the night's darkness. I'm sitting here curled up in my prayer chair, waking body, soul, and spirit. Mornings like this are such a reminder, a picture, a back-in-time of when darkness covered my life and glimpses of light began to break in. I know now it was You! I was seeing, sensing, being drawn into Your heart with glimpses of glory.

Dearest Dawn-Breaker,

I am here.

I have been waiting for you.

What would You like to talk about today?

Jesus ...: Are you *here in this place* hoping to be healed? (John 5:6).

Lord Jesus,

I'm here to meet with You. Yes, there are areas of concern for me and others, but they are secondary to my being with You. I sit here grateful for the deep healing body, soul, and spirit over these past several months.

I don't want this morning to be about me. I never want something I want to talk to You about to be more important that Who I am talking to. My heart is full to overflowing with the awareness that my God, the Holy One of Israel, is waiting to talk to me.

I sensed Jesus interrupting me and asking again,

Are you here in this place hoping to be healed?

I've noticed that Jesus often returns to the question at hand. In fact, a study of the Gospels reveals Jesus asked far more questions than were asked of Him. Accounting for differences in translations, Jesus asked about 350 questions. He was asked 180 questions, and He only answered three.

Why does Jesus ask so many questions? Because they make us search His heart for the answer. We dig through the Scriptures. We wait and listen. Seek. Knock. Ask. The Holy Spirit has a way of teaching us these integral facets of our prayer life.

As we follow Jesus into John 5, the first thing He is concerned about is the condition of our body, soul, and spirit. Oh, how I love the heart of the Father reflected in the Son. When we meet with God—whether it's morning, noon, or night; whether it's sitting in a car-pool lane, commuting to work, or waiting in a doctor's office—we come to Jesus, and He asks, "Are you here in this place hoping to be healed?"

In verses 6–8, Jesus has a conversation with the disabled man. I'm reminded that many are *disabled*, though perhaps not recognizably to the naked eye. Only the spiritual eye can see it. The enemy wants you to stay stuck in depression, fear of man, panic attacks, sleepless nights … the list can go on and on. I strongly sense that many of you need to pause here and have your own conversation with Jesus before you will be able hear "Stand up, carry your mat, and walk" (John 5:8).

Let me pray for you.

> Lord Jesus,
>   You see the secret place. The hidden pain. The buried past which becomes present. And You alone carry hope and healing. Yours is the reached-out hand for every one of us. Now, Lord, as one stops and cries out to You, hear their cry. Bring healing and wholeness to the places that are bound—the places You came to set free.

I began a fast to separate myself: to hear and obey, to listen and rethink, to renew my mind.

Dear Lord Jesus,
    I'm 33 days into this 40-day fast. Is there anything You would like me to add? I would like to continue. I really sense a hand-in-hand, follow Me grace on this fast. There is more I'm seeking—more breakthrough and understanding. I'm so careful, Lord, not to presume or make a religious act out of fasting. But I can't deny the freshness of Your presence and awareness of our partnership. I don't want to end this
        burning bush,
            tent of meeting,
                altar in my heart.
I'm so aware of how depleted I was and how graciously and gently Your goodness met me and carried me to this new place in Your heart.
How could I not
    press in
    and press on?

The tasks ahead are daunting. But somehow, hand in hand,
I'm filled with expectation and hope.

Dear One,

Pause. Let Me fill you. You are going to be pouring out a lot
these next days, and I will be right next to you, pouring in. At
times, I will pour in faster than you are pouring out. There
will be an overflow.

Those will be the life Spirit-led sidebars; it's-more-Me-than-
you times. Those moments are the joy, partnership, hand-in-
hand moments that give you and others life. Those moments
will mark this season in preparation for the next.

Jesus,

Sometimes (don't laugh) I know I get ahead of You. When
Your God-idea becomes more my good-idea. And it doesn't
take long for the idea to become dry,

duty,

drudgery.

I'm learning Your pace and rhythm as I follow You and walk
hand in hand. So this is what equally yoked is supposed to
look like!

Mary,

You wonder _____.

I'm saying _____.

You worry _____.

I'm saying _____.

You wait for _____.

I'm saying _____.

I know, and I'll let you know what you need to know when you
need to know it.

Love, your Bread of Life.

There is a holy exchange between God and us. I pray your journaling of these conversations has brought a new dimension to the listening aspect of prayer.

Faith Takes Hold

Early one morning, I found myself on my knees. Sometimes I'm one step forward and two steps back. Jesus was gently but firmly moving me forward into a new season. For His reason and my lifetime. But I still struggled with those inner voices that fought what Jesus was saying to me.

There's a reason I started this day on my knees next to my bed.
  Your mercies are new every morning. My *trying* yesterday left
  me tired. I need more of You, God.
You haven't thanked Me.
  You're right.
You haven't thanked Me.
  Thank You.
  Thank You.
  Really. Thank You.
What's important to you is important to Me.
Because
what's important to Me is important to you.
You didn't dream of _____ and _____.

> "For I know the plans I have for you," declares the Lord,
> "plans to prosper you and not to harm you, plans to give
> you hope and a future" (Jeremiah 29:11 NIV).

You didn't dream of _____ either.

I did.

And I have.

Often in spite of you.

Quit fighting Me.

Quit reading the last chapter first to "see if you like the ending."

Believe. Hear. Obey.

Hear. Believe. Obey.

I'm trying ...

You're doing good. Nothing—no time—wasted. Remember the royal official (John 4:26) who heard My voice and *faith took hold of him.*

Lord Jesus, hand in hand, I'll follow You.

Readers, can we agree on this? Once you surrendered your life to God, the adventure began. He has and wants to do more than you could dream or imagine. Let me say to you what I said to God:

Forgive me for making it so hard. Forgive me when my mind, will, and emotions fight against what I know my spirit knows and has come into agreement with You. Give me the courage to live outside my comfort zone. That's where You are. Amen.

Go ahead; I know you have something you want to talk to Jesus about. And I know He wants to listen and has something to say back to you.

The Truth Is

As a new Christian, I knew the Bible was foundational, a "light to my path"[1] part of my new life. I grew up hearing Scripture but was in no way a student of the Word. Holding my Bible, I would sit and stare at Genesis to Revelation—66 books, 1,189 chapters, 31,102 verses (KJV). I clearly remember being overwhelmed with a definite "Where do I start?" feeling. I also remember trusting others to know the Word, understand the Word, and communicate the Word much better than I could. So, for several years I hid behind their coats. I quoted them. I trusted their Holy Spirit more than mine. I became a Christian echo.

The truth is God wants each of us to be like the Bereans: those mentioned in Scripture as Jews who "received the word with all readiness, and searched the Scriptures daily *to find out* whether these things were so" (Acts 17:11 NKJV).

There is a great need in the Church for those who equip the saints—for apostles, prophets, pastors, teachers, and evangelists. For Bible teachers, mentors, and resources like books, podcasts, and conferences. We are so blessed that there is so much to feed the hungry sheep! Scores of generations have been taught apologetics by the writings of C. S. Lewis and present-day apologists. God has blessed many with an anointing to communicate biblical truths, which in return cause our hearts to burn (Luke 24:32). Time and again, I listen to or watch an anointed message and receive a new nugget, revelation, or understanding and an increased hunger,

---

[1] Psalm 119:105 NKJV.

not just to know the Word but also to have my heart, mind, and soul transformed, healed, and encouraged.

There is no question we need others. But others are *never* a substitute for personally delving into the conversation and allowing the Word to do what only it can do.

> For the word of God is alive and active. Sharper than any double-edged sword, it penetrates even to dividing soul and spirit, joints and marrow; it judges the thoughts and attitudes of the heart (Hebrews 4:12 NIV).

> All Scripture is God-breathed and is useful for teaching, rebuking, correcting and training in righteousness, so that the servant of God may be thoroughly equipped for every good work (2 Timothy 3:16–17 NIV).

So here we are in John 5:19. Jesus begins with "The truth is," and we sit and listen and absorb spirit and truth. Much like at the well, Jesus breaks the spirit of religion and introduces us to the truth of the Son of God who came to the earth for you and me. He ends with "believe in Me" (John 5:46).

> Show me Your ways, O Lord;
> Teach me Your paths.
> Lead me in Your truth and teach me
> (Psalm 25:4–5 NKJV).

The word *truth* in this Scripture speaks to certainty, rightness, and trustworthiness. It comes from a word meaning firm, permanent, and established. This is what the truth will do for you and me.

As you read, meditate. Take your time. Talk to the Lord, dig through Scriptures, and let Jesus ask you questions. Let this part of John 5 seal truth into your life like an oak tree, whose roots go deep into your spirit. No storm, controversy, naysayer, or false belief will be able to move you.

This is where I bow out for your conversation through these verses. This is where you sit at the Teacher's feet and listen. This is where you ponder and pray. The Spirit of wisdom and revelation will show you great and mighty things you may not fully understand. Allow the Scriptures to become seeds of truth buried deep into your spirit.

> Lord Jesus,
> I don't have to understand truth for it to be true. But as a follower of Yours, I desire not only to understand and believe but also to be strengthened by the truth of Your Word. Let it become a light to my path. Fill my mouth with wisdom and my heart with Your love.
> Teach me.

I know Jesus is calling out a pure, spotless Bride—the Church. That's you and me. And yet, because of the pace we keep, I often think of a bridezilla crawling down the aisle to meet her Bridegroom. That's not the picture God has in mind for His Church, nor is it His plan. We are about to walk into a new chapter and discover exactly what *about my Father's business* means. And stay with me—there's a surprise yumminess at the end.

Somewhere in this task-driven highway of constant information, filled with so many good God-things to do, there eventually comes a STOP! Ironically, my doctor's office has a blue sign the exact shape of a stop sign, and it reads, "BREATHE."

Scripture not only invites but also commands us to stop. *Stop.* Breathe. Rest. Whatever direction you are going in, whatever path you are on, wherever you are in your journey—if you are lagging behind or running head of God, you will run into a stop sign. God will get your attention. *Stop* is so much better than a dead-end. Lean into John 6. There are a variety of conversations Jesus wants to have with you. Pull over to the side of your busy highway, find a rest stop, and listen to His heart for you.

JOHN 6

My Father's Business

Jesus,
Our life moments keep me going.
Today, however, I press pause. These past weeks have been
busy and much of it "about my Father's business," yet there's
a sense of getting ahead of myself. I can get so "forest for
the trees" thinking. It's too important that I give You every
opportunity to reset, renew, or realign my thinking. Instead
of looking for the fruit when often times it's a planting/
watering season, I need to sit. Wait. Listen.

Mary,
I know what's in your heart. I put those dreams, desires, and
directions there. But now look at what I've put in your heart
and in your hands.

Jesus (*to Philip*): Where is a place to buy bread so these people may
eat? (John 6:5).

When I ask you this question, I'm speaking of the Bread of My
presence that abides in you. On your own, it would only
serve a few. By My Spirit, however, it will serve multitudes.
The *what* is in you. The *how* is up to Me.

Make bread. Bake bread. Serve bread. Spiritually. And for you
… literally. The people whom you serve will come, will be
drawn, to the abiding presence of My Spirit. You be you, and
I'll be Me. It's that easy.

I know what I am planning. "Oh, the plans I have for you ..."
  I'm asking you to get you and Me on the same page.
  Fresh manna each day.
  Manna for today.
  Double portion manna for Sabbath rest.

> Jesus knew what He was planning to do, but He asked
> Philip nonetheless. He had something to teach, and it
> started with a test (John 6:6).

This doesn't surprise me. Does it you? We are often tested
by the Spirit of God. Thankfully, most of the time I know it's a
test, and I think, "I can do this. I can pass this test." Then there
are times I think the enemy is attacking me from the north,
south, east, and west, but no—it's God testing and strengthening me in the process. Test. Such a word! Is there anything
God wants to talk to you about in regard to *testing*? Anything
you have to ask? I am grateful we have a forgiving and persistent
God, and our eternity is not met with a report card. But oh
how I want to pass my earthly tests and draw closer to Him.
Identifying these tests and teachings allows for a godly response
on our part: "Lord, I want to pass this test. Teach me what You
will. Amen."

Often, Lord, my labors and laboring in prayer produce
        only crumbs.
        Not even enough for a meal.
Mary, I am God.
  I can and will do so much with what you surmise as so little.
  Often, these times are tests of the heart. The motive.
        The agenda.
  Often, it is a maturing and purifying time.

In these times, I am teaching.
In these times of testing and teaching, My desire for you is to hear and obey.
I've watched your struggles with delay. I've heard your cries for others. I am watching over My Word to perform it.

Time for me to start mining for gold, searching the Scriptures. In this case, it was the word *test*. In my *Spirit-Filled Life* Bible, I found this:

> **tested**, *peirazo* … The word describes the testing of the believer's loyalty, strength, opinions, disposition, condition, faith, patience or character. *Peirazo* determines which way one is going and what one is made of.[1]

I feel impressed to stop here. There is a word of exhortation welling up for you.

> There are many people, projects, and prayers that are leftover. When I think of leftovers, I immediately think of food not consumed from a meal. The food is still good. It still has value. It still can feed and nourish the body.
>
> There are leftover people, projects, and prayers that God will have you collect and complete. Some were out of season. They were left, neglected, or stored away. They were hopes deferred. They were passed on from another generation or passed over by this generation.
>
> Luke 14:16–24 tells the story of a man who prepared a great feast and invited many guests. However, everyone declined, each person using a different excuse. Finally, the man told his slave:

---

[1] Jack Hayford, ed., *Spirit-Filled Life Bible* (Nashville, TN: Thomas Nelson, 1991), 1820.

"Go out at once into the streets and lanes of the city and bring in here the poor and crippled and blind and lame." And the slave said, "Master, what you commanded has been done, and still there is room." And the master said to the slave, "Go out into the highways and along the hedges, and compel *them* to come in, so that my house may be filled" (Luke 14:21–23 NASB).

God is saying, "I'm compelling you by the Spirit; *now* is the time to collect and complete." I'm praying for you to hear Him clearly about leftovers. Pick up your pen and begin writing: books, songs, blogs, notes, etc. Write to whomever the Lord brings to your mind—spouse, family members, friends, ministry partners, etc. Renew commitments, rebuild friendships, and restore relationships.

Stewardship

As I travelled through John 6, I celebrated my 37th year as a disciple of Jesus Christ. I'm so sentimental about my anniversaries with Jesus. It's because I clearly remember life without Him. I wrote a lot of my testimony in *Adventures in Prayer*. The "before" was not pretty. I was sad and lost and hurting. I had no friends. Notta. Zero. I lived away from family and had a wonderful, exciting job. But friends? No. Honestly, I could go a full weekend and need to say words out loud just to hear a voice speak.

But God ...

So, yes, I'm sentimental and grateful beyond words. I have a deep desire to count my days and make them count for Him!

Year 37. Only three years from 40! I love being intentional about time and dates. This may be one reason I love the

Jewish feasts and calendars so much. Each one is so intentional. Meaningful. A compass to my journey.

When my dear friend Pastor Tim Ross turned 37, he set a course for his 40th year. He got off social media. He put all his books aside, except for the Bible. He set out to seek Jesus with his whole heart, soul, mind, and time! I was inspired. I decided to talk to Jesus and get His thoughts as I made a three-year plan of my own.

Tick Tock Tick Tock Tick Tock
Hours. Days. Weeks. Months. Marching by.
Are You sensing my desire, Lord,
 to be intentional about a three-year plan?
To march into my 40th anniversary,
that marks my end and Your beginning of
 this surrendered heart
  to Your loving hands?
Today, Lord, an opportunity to not so much look back; rather,
 look forward.
Where do You want me spiritually in three years?
 And what are the steps to get there?
  Be there?
I know You asked me
 Where do I want to be?
 What would I like to accomplish?
  In my private walk?
  In my public walk?
   In my preparation to see You face-to-face?
    Love,
    Mary

Dear One,
    I know your heart. And I say,
        Stewardship!

Whoa! I needed to look up that word and spend some time meditating on stewardship. The Holy Spirit put a list of ideas on my heart:

- planning and managing resources
- overseeing and protecting something worth caring for and preserving
- working with my own hands (1 Corinthians 4:12)
- using my talents (Matthew 25:14–30)
- multiplying
  - time
  - talent
  - testimony
  - treasure

So, Beloved One,
    My plan is to *steward* you. My Father gave you to Me, and when I present you to Him, I will give Him back My treasure.
I will steward you as you steward people, situations, circumstances, prayers, plans, and purposes I entrust to you.
Together.
Love, Jesus

Oh my! Have you ever thought of Jesus stewarding you for this purpose and in this way? I hadn't. Time to journal. What do you think? What is the Holy Spirit saying to you?

So … what I'm hearing You say …

What You're saying, Jesus, is You are going to plan and manage me, and I am Your *resource.*

That You will be responsible to oversee and protect me.

That I am worth caring for and preserving.

I know You, Lord, to be trustworthy. I know You to multiply the resources in me. I know You have redeemed the time in my life, and You've used talents I didn't even know I had. I want my testimony to be used by You to *overcome* however You desire, and the treasure will be the crown I lay at Your feet.

And then I had to press a little and ask a brave question:

My question: What do You consider my greatest resource?

Love.

The way you love Me.

And the way you love others through Me.

Love.

Where do I start? Or where do You want to start?

Mary, what's in your hand?

I have a dream, a desire, a direction. I want to _____.

Go do it, Daughter. My hands will be on your shoulders.

You'll be looking over my shoulder?

That's right! I'm removing the burdens you are carrying, and I'm replacing them with the yolk of assurance that I am with you. I have your back. Remember the yolk is worn/carried on the shoulders. And I have declared your burdens are light. You have rolled all your cares and concerns upon Me. I will cause your thoughts to become agreeable with My will for this

_____.

Thank You, Lord Jesus. Thank You, Redeemer. Thank You, Shepherd.

Friends, I must tell you that many of my journal pages have tears on them. This was one of those times. Please take as much time as you need and Jesus wants. He's going to speak to you about stewarding you! How special. How personal. How eternal.

Jesus gave me this picture, and it won't go away—the time when I do meet Him face-to-face and He hands me back to the Father as someone He *personally stewarded*. I don't know about you, but I love the thought.

Equally Yoked

You may have noticed a phrase I've used a couple times: *equally yoked*. Most often we hear this phrase when speaking about young people waiting for the right spouse. It refers to marrying someone who shares a common faith, core beliefs, value system, and moral compass. All good counsel.

But what about being equally yoked to Jesus in prayer? Letting Him carry the burden as we come alongside in agreement. As in "Come to Me, all who are weary and heavy-laden, and I will give you rest" (Matthew 11:28 NASB).

Intercessory assignments can become downright burdensome. Heartbreaking even. God is the only answer or solution—the only way out. Many times we find ourselves carrying the prayer need to the point it becomes unrighteous. In other words, we put the burden of the answer on us praying long enough, hard enough, and loud enough. *Did I pray right? Did I pray boldly, confidently, and with enough faith?*

These are indications that your prayer life is not balanced. Stay equally yoked to Jesus. Remain in the Word. Ask the Father how He wants you to pray. Be led by the Spirit and not your mind, will, or emotions. Prayer is always a matter of the heart. Check your heart. Keep it strong in the Lord.

Several years ago, I received a prophetic word that resonated with me and became a measuring rod as I grew in my prayer and intercessory assignments:

> Do you know the difference between a righteous and unrighteous burden?
>
> Don't let it ever become a burden and put any more expectations on yourself than God is putting on you. I think there has been a time in the past where the Lord says you have put expectations on yourself and the ministry that God has placed on your heart that He didn't put there. And you have found yourself struggling in a yoke that God was not in with you. The Lord says that every yoke He ever places on you is a double yoke, and He is doing all the pulling; we are just along for the ride. And the Lord wants to remind you to just be along for the ride. It's His hand upon you that does the calling. Don't do a lot of the pulling anymore. If the burden you place on yourself becomes too much, the Lord will withdraw His ministry from you just because He cares for you.
>
> He is going to release you to new levels only when it becomes a joy to you; only when it is never a burden; only when you can go to sleep at night and sleep soundly. As you develop that tendency in you to release it to Him, don't worry, don't fear, and don't let it become a burden.

You know the difference between the righteous and unrighteous burden.

The righteous shall flourish like a palm tree,
He shall grow like a cedar in Lebanon.
Those who are planted in the house of the Lord,
Shall flourish in the courts of our God.
They shall still bear fruit in old age;
They shall be fresh and flourishing,
To declare that the Lord is upright;
He is my rock, and *there is* no unrighteousness in Him
(Psalm 92:12–15 NKJV).

Jesus wants to keep reminding you and me that we are not alone. He mediated for us on the cross, declared, "It is finished!" and now ever lives to make a way for us to mediate for others.

Bread of Life

So much of my own journey was about internal transformation: perceptions, ideas, and mindsets. Giving intentional time to listen to Jesus address body, soul, and spirit in my life. This season required leaning in and trusting Him on a new level; not through the lenses of what worked yesterday but rather what He wanted to do in me now. Jesus wanted to move me to new places of worship, prayer, and service—all with eternity in mind.

Jesus,
Somewhere along the way, I went from wrestling to resting,
   from wondering to revelation,
   from worrying to renewing body, soul, and spirit.

Somewhere, perhaps when You were speaking to the Pharisee in me, maybe at the wedding feast, or even at the well … Somewhere along the way, I've gone from a season of fear to not being afraid. So in John 6:20, when You tell me that You are the ONE and not to be afraid, I can look over my shoulder at what was and look forward with a new set, settled, and secure confidence in following You.

Mary,

Jesus: I tell you the truth (John 6:26).

We have talked about bread and manna and feeding the sheep. But now we will talk about the bread that gives life—eternal life. An earthly perspective, a here and now, what-do-I-need-to-do-to-get-through-today mentality to an eternal kingdom, heaven-to-earth view.

Three times in John 6, Jesus says, "I tell you the truth" and then gives us food that is eternal. Not bread-from-heaven manna like Moses gave. Not manna for a day. Not manna that will waste away. Rather, manna that will stay—the bread of God that our Father offers.

In Exodus 25 we learn about the *bread of the presence,* which was the showbread in the tabernacle of Moses. This bread was always in the Lord's presence. John 6 reveals that Jesus now offers Himself as our bread:

Jesus: I am the bread that gives life. If you come to My table and eat, you will never go hungry. Believe in Me, and you will never go thirsty (John 6:35).

Never hungry. Never thirsty. Just as He offered living water to the woman at the well, Jesus offers Himself to us.

Jesus took bread, and when he had given thanks, he broke it and gave it to his disciples, saying, "Take and eat; this is my body" (Matthew 26:26 NIV).

Continual. Communion. Commandment.

Lord,

These Scriptures challenge me. First, Jesus, to reflect again on the ultimate sacrifice You made to come to earth with no agenda but to do the will of Your Father. And the deep revelation of the Trinity: Father, Jesus, Holy Spirit—God in three, blessed unity. My prayer life and my communion with You is taken to a whole new level of intimacy and power in Your presence when I pray the will of the Father in the abiding presence of Jesus and through the power of the Holy Spirit.

Will. Word. Works.

Mary, this is *key* to our relationship and partnership. Let's talk …

The next several conversations were spent meditating on these Scriptures.

Continual

One of my prayer non-negotiables is *time with God in my prayer chair.* This holy spiritual discipline has created a pace and rhythm in my life that results in me being strengthened body, soul, and spirit. Daily manna.

This continual meeting with God has become an anchor and a compass in my life. Life from this place overflows into every relationship and conversation—everything I do and all that I am. Manna. Daily. My life Scripture is Psalm 17:15:

> As for me, Father, because of Jesus' righteousness and my right standing with You, I will be fully satisfied when I awake in the morning, seeing You face-to-face and having sweet *communion* with You (MJP).

Communion

Exodus 33 shares intimate conversations between God and Moses as they speak face-to-face. God promises that His presence will travel with Moses, and He will give him rest. Then Moses confirms, "If your presence is not going with us, don't make us leave this place" (Exodus 33:15 GW). He had already come to the revelation that God's presence was imperative for hearing and obeying God. Moses was willing, but God's presence made him able.

Both words, *presence* and *face,* are the same Hebrew word. Daily time in His presence cultivates "My Presence will go *with you,* and I will give you rest" (Exodus 33:14 NKJV).

Commandment

As you read, meditate, and engage Jesus in your personal conversation through these Scriptures, I invite you to consider practical, pragmatic, and powerful ways you can engage the Bread of Life in your daily life.

The most inspiring principle that has taught me about Jesus being the *Bread of Life and the abiding presence of God* has been

my quest to incorporate the goodly gift of Sabbath into my life.
I say "goodly gift" because of a quote from the Talmud:

> Said The Holy One, Blessed Be He to Moses:
> Moses, in my storehouse I have a goodly gift,
> and the Sabbath is its name.[2]

> Thus God blessed day seven and made it special—*an
> open time for pause and restoration, a sacred zone of
> Sabbath-keeping,* because God rested from all the work
> He had done in creation that day (Genesis 2:3).

Several years ago, challenged to figure out what Sabbath
really looked like in my life, I discovered one of the hidden
treasures of the special, set-apart holy day. And of all places,
I found it in my kitchen! I learned that a key to a traditional
Jewish Sabbath meal is Challah (sounds like "ha-la")—a beautifully intricate and rich braided loaf of bread—so I decided to
make it.

I thought, "I can do this! What's so complicated about a little
flour, water, eggs, and yeast?" Thankfully, I found the entire
process to be very forgiving, friendly, and just plain fun!

My first attempt was comical. But lost in the flour mess
and watching the yeast bubble, I tapped into a wonder and
awe watching the ingredients all work together. And in a short
amount of time, my house was filled with the wonderful aroma
of freshly baked bread and my heart with a warm "well done."
Oh, I wish you could smell the yumminess through these pages.

Now, I bake Challah every week as part of my Sabbath. (I've
included the recipe for my Honey Challah in the appendix.) I
listen to worship music as I mix the ingredients and wait for

---

[2] Talmud, *Beitzah* 16a.

them to rise, and I meet with the Lord. Then I share my newly baked masterpiece with family and friends, bonding over its goodness while we bless the Lord and one another.

I've discovered the gifts of rest, worship, prayer, fun, hospitality, and mentoring through this simple act. The hidden treasure is in the unassuming, unforced rhythm of the baking process. The secret of the Sabbath is slowing down and changing your normal hectic pace by praying, worshipping, and honoring God. And each time I bake bread, I find rest. I come away full physically but hungry spiritually. It's funny how one loaf of bread can transform how I rest, live, pray, and understand Scripture. I tell my worship-leading friends that baking bread is my guitar or piano. *I need to knead.*

It's often said the more you make bread, the more you will get to know how it is supposed to look and feel as you mix and knead it. But I have discovered just the opposite. The more I mix and knead and bake, the more God shows me new things about tradition, family, blessing, and Sabbath rest. And the more I find others who are hungry as well—not only for bread but also for the joy of baking and rest. I've gathered hundreds in my kitchen—men, women, and children—and together we've laughed and prayed around a simple loaf. It's ageless, it's genderless, it's timeless, and it binds us together. I am certain that when we reach heaven, the Lord Himself will gather us all for a meal in His presence. And you know there will be bread on His table.

JOHN 7

Staff of Life

Each chapter in John offers a lifetime of conversations with the Lord. Worship. Prayer. Warfare. Intercession. Declarations. Convictions. A lifetime of falling deeper in love with Jesus over and over again. Fresh manna. New revelation. His presence lifts off the pages of the Bible like sweet incense. Of course, chapter 7 has its own gifts wrapped up in the red-letter words.

John 7 begins, "After these events, *it was time for Jesus to move on*" (v. 1). And saints, this is the case for you and me. Let's move on to see what Jesus wants to talk about, challenge us, and charge us with as we walk into today with Him.

Dear Lord Jesus,
  What a whirlwind these past weeks have been. I'm so grateful
  You're speaking about life and life eternal and trusting
   and resting in You. It has really made a difference in my
   decision-making.
  When people
    and plans
    and ideas
    and commitments
    and calendar
      keep trying to squeeze You out of my day, mind,
      actions, and reactions, I find myself defaulting to
      the non-negotiables You are building into my prayer
      life—into my living prayer with You. As I follow You

through these Scriptures and conversations, I'm left pondering and living a lot more like Mary than Martha.

On this 15-day trip to 3 countries (6 flights, 2 trains, buses, vans, 3 conferences, and 15 friends), there was a constant assurance You were with me.

A highlight of this trip was saying "no" to something good and "yes" to something God. The day I listened and obeyed. The day I turned down visiting some amazing places with some wonderful people because You wanted to talk. It was my favorite day. Our most special meeting. Thank you.[1]

Mary,

I'm so aware of your inner turmoil over details,
decisions, and
deadlines.

Remember:

> "But *only* one thing is necessary, for Mary has chosen the good part, which shall not be taken away from her" (Luke 10:42 NASB).

I will continue to give you opportunities to choose the *good part*. Do not let the distractions and attempted detours or delays rob you.

Choose the main thing: Me.

That will never be taken from you. My presence will go with you. The day you sacrificed and stayed back from touring Poland was My favorite day too. You chose the better part. **Being** in the right place at the right time is *key* to following Me.

---

[1] I wrote about this day in *Adventures in Prayer*, Day 37: Warsaw Prayer Meeting.

Jesus: ... I am not going *right now* because My time is not yet at hand (John 7:8).

Timing is key to being at the right place at the right time. After four decades of serving the Lord, I was asked, "Looking back, what is one bit of wisdom or advice you would give someone?" Immediately, I responded, "I wouldn't let my passion get ahead of His purposes." The clarity and quickness of my answer surprised me! I knew it was from God's heart that I spoke. Our passion for serving, for souls, for salvations, for the Church, for loved ones, and for hearing "Well done, good and faithful servant" can easily get us out of sync with the timing of God.

Jesus demonstrated over and over again how timing positions us for God's purposes to be accomplished and for His power to break through the most hardened, dark, impossible situations.

Here in John 7, Jesus addresses the most important element of partnership with Him. It's not where or what or how or why. Rather, it's **who.**

Jesus clearly knew who He was and what His mission was. He was tethered to the will of the Father and filled and empowered with the Holy Spirit. He was God *and* man. When exactly did this knowing, this revelation, come in full? The Bible doesn't say. Was it as a young boy as He learned the Scriptures? When He taught the rabbis or questioned His timing with His Mother? Was it when He was baptized and came out of the water hearing, "This is My beloved Son, in whom I am well pleased" (Matthew 17:5 NKJV)? Was it during the 40 days of fasting? We just don't know.

But this we do know: Jesus came to a full realization of who He was and what He was on earth to accomplish.

Though he was God,
> he did not think of equality with God
> as something to cling to.
Instead, he gave up his divine privileges;
> he took the humble position of a slave
> and was born as a human being.
When he appeared in human form,
> he humbled himself in obedience to God
> and died a criminal's death on a cross
> (Philippians 2:6–8 NLT).

There are dozens of quotes about becoming like the people with whom you keep company. Proverbs says,

> He who walks with wise *men* will be wise,
> But the companion of fools will be destroyed
> (Proverbs 13:20 NKJV).

Through the Scriptures, we get to walk with the wisest Man who ever lived. Following closely and covered with the Rabbi's dust, we see how He loved, lived, served, and spoke. What was important to Him becomes important to us. Look at the conversations you've had with Jesus. See how loving and patient and kind He is—how merciful and generous and grace-filled in drawing you near. How wisely and consistently He leads.

- Humble
- Servant Leader
- Committed
- Patient
- Long-Suffering

And *always* pointing us to the Father.

Jesus: I do not claim ownership of My words; they are *a gift* from the One who sent Me.... I chase only after glory for the One who sent Me. My intention is *authentic and* true. You'll find no wrong *motives* in Me (John 7:16, 18).

Lord Jesus,
Over and over again, You direct me to the Father. Over and over again, You call to mind,

> "If you want to boast, boast only about the Lord"
> (2 Corinthians 10:17 NLT).

Oh Lord,
Break what needs to be broken.
Heal what needs to be healed.
Make me whole in You
that I may be as authentic and true.
Cleanse me from any wicked motives or ways.
Increase as I decrease.

Dear One,
You remind Me of Jacob. Remember that long night of transformation? By My grace and mercy, he went from "deceiver" (fearful, long-suffering) to receiving a new name, nature, and purpose. He became the man he was created to be: a man of faith, love, and goodness. He left that night leaning on a staff for the rest of his life.

> By faith Jacob, when he was dying, blessed each of
> Joseph's sons, and worshiped as he leaned on the top of
> his staff (Hebrews 11:21 NIV).

Oh, Lord Jesus, a staff! Jesus, You are my staff!
Staff of life is bread. Bread is Your presence.

May I always and forever, like Song of Solomon, come up from this
wilderness leaning on my Beloved. Lord Jesus, put a seal over my
heart "like a seal on your arm" (Song of Solomon 8:6 NLT).
I am Yours.
I am Yours.
I am Yours.
My Beloved!
May I always and forever lean on You, my Beloved.
Selah. Pause. Think on this.

Leaning on the walls of my office and prayer room are literal
staffs—prophetic pieces of art crafted at the hands of a dear
friend, a modern-day Bezalel. He sees dead pieces of wood and
creates a living voice of God, calling many to walk out of the
wilderness by leaning on Jesus, our Staff of Life.

My ministry staff consists of two different pieces of wood,
joined together in one strong, unbreakable bond. On the staff
are two sets of 12 circles representing the 12 tribes of Israel
and the 12 apostles. These two sets of 12 became significant as
my love for Israel grew, and the one new man (Ephesians 2:15)
prayer and intercession arose in me. Combined, they make 24:
the number of elders worshipping before the throne of God
in Revelation. My staff is a reminder of prayer and worship
coming together in ministry and in my life.

God continues to ask, "What is in your hand?" Today He
speaks of the Staff of Life—the Lord Jesus Himself, my Beloved
whom I continually lean on. From here to eternity.

Mary,
You are grafted into My love, plans, and purposes. Keep leaning.
Keep depending. Keep trusting.

I am your Keeper! (Psalm 121:5–6 NKJV).

Dear readers,

Like Jesus:

- We need to know what we know.
- We need to be confident of who God is and who we are as rightful heirs.
- We need to have a sure foundation of our faith.
- We need to know what we believe.
- We need to live from a place of our inheritance in Christ.

  Son.

  Daughter.

Settled

During the formative years of my faith, I memorized several prayers, one of which was the Apostle's Creed. I have always loved reciting this prayer.

I believe in God, the Father almighty,
creator of heaven and earth.
I believe in Jesus Christ, God's only Son, our Lord,
who was conceived by the Holy Spirit,
born of the Virgin Mary,
suffered under Pontius Pilate,
was crucified, died, and was buried;
he descended to the dead.
On the third day he rose again;
he ascended into heaven,
he is seated at the right hand of the Father,

and he will come to judge the living and the dead.
I believe in the Holy Spirit,
the holy catholic Church,
the communion of saints,
the forgiveness of sins,
the resurrection of the body,
and the life everlasting. Amen.

Lord,
There's a part of this well You're digging in me that is hungry
and thirsty for a rhythm of faith that is foundational to
who I am and what I believe. Thank You for bringing to my
remembrance this prayer, memorized as a young girl, that
draws a boundary line around my faith. My faith is a pleasant
place, and it is my inheritance (Psalm 16:5–6).

I am grateful for Glenn Packiam's book *Discover the Mystery
of Faith*.[2] I highly recommend it to anyone wanting to know
more about the creeds and songs of the early Church and how
they relate to our worship today. The world may attempt
to alter or manipulate what faith looks like, but even in the
modern sea of religious uncertainty, the truth of these prayers
serves as an anchor for our faith. Century after century, they
still offer life and breath to the soul.

Lord,
The more I revisit the footprints of this journey through John,
the more aware I am of how Your presence will lead me.

---

[2] Glenn Packiam, *Discover the Mystery of Faith* (Colorado Springs: David C
Cook, 2013).

I want to be in the right place at the right time.
I want to say the right things at the right time.
I want to represent You well here on earth,
　　As You represented well the Father in heaven.
You're such a wonderful Shepherd. I love being one of Your
　　sheep who *hears Your voice and follows.*
Dear Jesus,
　　You were always so certain of who You were and what You
　　were about. So
　　　　　　set,
　　　　　settled,
　　　　secure.

This is exactly what a dear pastor prayed for me: that I would become set, settled, and secure in what God was asking of me. The longer I lingered and listened in John 7, the more settled my spirit became. The situations didn't change, and the circumstances were not altered. The prayer burdens for loved ones and friends and the Church were still there. Some even intensified. But I was more *settled.*

Thank You, Jesus.
Mary,
　　I knew where I came from.
　　I knew where I was going (John 7:33).
And Mary,
　　I know where you came from,
　　And I know where you are going.
Follow Me.
Dear Lord,
Pausing. Taking time for worship and prayer. Do You have

any idea how full my heart is? How grateful I am for Your coming to earth to save me from myself? But also for showing me how to live and love and serve. If I were like David, with the gift of scripting eternal words of praise and thanksgiving, I would do just that. Here, Lord: my praise and thanksgiving for the rivers of living water You have flowing through me.

I slowly left John 7, holding tightly to every word, promise, and prayer and pressing forward to John 8.

JOHN 8

Lay Down Your Stone

Few biblical characters are easier for readers to identify with than the woman caught in adultery. Not necessarily because of her specific sin, but because of the humiliation any sin brings upon oneself. We all could finish the statement: "caught in _____." Whether we are caught in sin or convicted by it, the result is still the same—condemnation. Either others condemn us, or we condemn ourselves.

However, if we are willing, we too can come face-to-face with a compassionate, forgiving, truth-speaking God.

We can relate to these verses—these images of the woman being accused and condemned for all to witness. I grieve for the repentant whose sins are headlines and fodder for others, often family, friends, and even the Church, to stone and condemn. I grieve for the wounded, weary, and battled-fatigued sinner, whose shame keeps him locked up and chained to the past.

> All have sinned and *continually* fall short of the glory of God (Romans 3:23 AMP).

You. Me. He. She. Them. Brother. Sister. Mother. Father. Friend. Husband. Wife. *All.*

And yet ...

All have access to Jesus. *All* have entrance to the throne of grace. *All* have the invitation, "Come to Me, you who are weary and sin-laden" (Matthew 11:28 MJP).

And then to those with ready and willing stones in their hands:

Jesus: Let the first stone be thrown by the one among you who has not sinned (John 8:7).

Are you holding a stone? Are you aiming at someone or even yourself? Jesus releases you from the unenviable position of judge and jury. I have found the very best prayer to pray is:

> Father, how can I pray for _____? Father, give me wisdom—Your heart, Your eyes, Your ears—to hear and see and let my prayers bring healing to _____.

What person or situation do you need to write into these blanks? Perhaps it is someone in a leadership position. Perhaps it is someone who was only in your life for a short time. Or maybe the blanks have your own name. Self-condemnation and self-hate will lead to stoning yourself.

But that is not God's way. Jesus made the way. He is the way, the truth, and the life (John 14:6).

Dear Lord,
There is no better time than today—right now—to have this conversation. The stone has become a rock of offense, and I want to build a stone of remembrance. I desire to lay this stone down and walk away free from judging others and being judged.
Dear Mary,
Where is everyone? *Are we alone?* (John 8:10).
Dear Lord,
Thank You for removing those arrows from my heart and

even my back. Thank You for giving me a safe place, here
with You.

Alone.

Somehow I picture You bending down and writing my
name in the sand.

My name … How personal. How You see me. How
intentional.

Somehow I see You standing and looking at me
face-to-face, and Your words, "I do not condemn you
either" leave me speechless but hopeful!

And faith is deposited.

Now faith is confidence in what we hope for and
assurance about what we do not see
(Hebrews 11:1 NIV).

Now to avoid going around this mountain again! Jesus gives
us the *how* to move forward:

"*All I ask is that you* go and from now on avoid the sins
that plague you" (John 8:11).

Lord,
Following You gives me the confidence that I can and will avoid
falling into the trap of condemning and judging others as well
as the sins that plagued me.
That's My way, Mary.

Jesus is very specific: we must avoid sins. But how can we do
this?

- Ask the Holy Spirit to highlight snares that have bound
  you in the past.
- Record what He says. Hear and obey.

Thrive

Jesus: I am the light that shines through the cosmos; if you walk with Me, you will thrive in the *nourishing* light that gives life and will not know darkness (John 8:12).

Challenged to see light in the darkness,
To discern how to shine His light into dark hearts,
To pray for His light on my path ,
The grace to live in this dark world and be His light.

Mary,
My will for you is to thrive, not just survive.

Thrive. That's a word with great promise.

Jesus,
My prayer is that I thrive, and so often I feel like I'm barely keeping my head above water.

I looked up the definition of *thrive*. Listen to this:

- to remain alive even after the death of something
- to endure or live through

Let's be John 8:12 and thrive in the nourishing light of Jesus. Let us remain alive as we die to mindsets, strongholds, or patterns that merely cause us to survive.

Let's be 1 Corinthians 13:7 and bear all things, believe all things, hope all things, and endure all things by thriving in Jesus.

Jesus is inviting you into a conversation about thriving in Him, through Him, and with Him. Don't miss this opportunity. Pause, pray, ponder, and journal your footsteps forward as you learn to thrive.

I AM

Jesus: …Unless you believe I am who I have said I am"
(John 8:24).

Lord,

I've always believed. I've always understood You as the one true God. I've always trusted You as God who became man. I've always known the Trinity—three in one. God the Father, God the Son, and God the Holy Spirit. As a child, I was prayed for, prayed over, and prayed with. There was never a question that You created the earth and all that is in it. And You created me.

And yet Lord, as I grew in faith, I was more aware of sin in my life. I wrestled. I fought. And I often lost the battle with the enemy of my soul. Like the father in Mark 9:24, I have cried, "I believe; help my unbelief!" (ESV).

Let Me talk.

Did you hear the last two words of that Scripture (John 8:24a): "I AM"?

I AM a bigger God than you know Me to be.

I AM more than you allow Me to be.

I AM greater than you even want Me to be. I AM.

Oh Lord,

I am so grateful we are not racing through the Gospel of John. I need the pauses. I need the pondering. I need the …

In Exodus 3, Moses asks God what name he should give if the Israelites ask who sent him. God replies, "'I AM THAT I AM' … say unto the children of Israel, 'I AM hath sent me unto you'" (Exodus 3:14 KJV).

In the Gospel of John, Jesus completes the I AM given to Moses:

- "I am the bread of life" (John 6:35 NIV).
- "I am the light of the world" (John 8:12 NIV).
- "I am the gate" (John 10:9 NIV).
- "I am the good shepherd" (John 10:11 NIV).
- "I am the resurrection and the life" (John 11:25 NIV).
- "I am the way and the truth and the life" (John 14:6 NIV).
- "I am the true vine" (John 15:1 NIV).

Mary,

I want you to know the whole of who I am. And not just know about. I want you to experience and live, having received all of who I am in your life.

Mary, I'm glad we stopped and talked.

Reread and refresh.

Revisit and reboot.

Renew and remember.

Yes, Lord, me too!

These early mornings are so special—a great time to meet and talk about the I AMs. Thank You for doing in me things I cannot do on my own. Thank You for the grace to walk upright and keep going. Thank You for the personal and powerful way You talk to me.

face to face

in your

Tentology – study of meeting with God

Tent of

away from
the
busyness
of camp
"LIFE"

Meeting

EXODUS 33:7-18

MOED - HEBREW
APPOINTED
· TIME
· MEETING
· PLACE
TENT OF MEETING !

Be INTENTIONAL

"Adonai, who can rest in
Your tent?" PSALM 15:1

Give me
your hands

I trust You—
Psalm 25

LET ME

hold
heal
fill
strengthen

YOU

Aaron & Hur
keeping hands Exodus 17:12

"I am the Lord your
God who takes hold
of your right hand.
Do not fear, I will help
you." Isaiah 41:13

Clean hands: Pure Heart

Nature of a Servant

Jesus
hands

BLESSED

Charged ————

Commanded ————

Commissioned

Christ —
Anointed One

Thomas—doubted

"Blessed are those
who never see Me & yet still
believe." John 20:29

JUST IMAGINE

Jesus

Stewarding

ME!

multiply — oversight — His plans —

The 'Question —
Will I let Him?

My time & talents
dreams & desires
resources & rest —

Prayer: O Lord, through
you, I will become a
faithful & wise
steward. Amen

LUKE 12:42

These conversations about the whole of You … something
shifted in my mind, my heart, and my spirit.
Mary,
When I say,

> "You shall know the truth, and the truth shall make you
> free" (John 8:32 NKJV),

it means just this. The truth of who I AM. The truth of the
Scriptures. The truth of your Father in heaven. The truth of
the Spirit of God.
This Scripture is so often taken out of context. This is not the
truth the world offers: the news media, the social media, the
entertainment media … any media. This is the truth of the
I AM.
Peace I leave with you; my peace I give you. I do not give to
you as the world gives. Do not let your hearts be troubled
and do not be afraid (John 14:27 paraphrase).
And JOY unspeakable.
You're ready to move forward. I'm so proud of you.
Thank You, Lord. What a mighty God I serve!
I love You.
And I love you.

It seems fitting that we pause and praise.

> Blessed *is* the man
> Who walks not in the counsel of the ungodly,
>   Nor stands in the path of sinners,
>   Nor sits in the seat of the scornful;
> But his delight *is* in the law of the Lord,
>   And in His law he meditates day and night.

He shall be like a tree
    Planted by the rivers of water,
    That brings forth its fruit in its season,
    Whose leaf also shall not wither;
And whatever he does shall prosper
    (Psalm 1:1–3 NKJV).

JOHN 9

Time

Time: that precious commodity you cannot buy, borrow, or get back; that which we constantly find ourselves wrestling and contending for.

Dear Lord,
In the busyness of life … Ugh! I even hate saying that word. "Busyness."

How often have you heard or even said, "I know you are busy, but …" That is one of the most heart-pained comments people say to me. I am busy—but not any busier than you! And different seasons are filled with different kinds of busyness.

When I teach on my three non-negotiables of living prayer, I address *busyness.* And the truth is there is no season in life when we are not *busy.* Young. Old. Student. Employee. Newly married. Parents. Retired. There is never a time when the world won't make you as busy as you allow it. By the way, Brady Boyd wrote a wonderful book, *Addicted to Busy.*[1] It addresses the value of establishing a not-too-busy mindset with God, which overflows to a not-too-busy "when passing by" like Jesus did when he met the blind man.

Busyness can be addressed successfully by applying these non-negotiables to your prayer life:

---

[1] Brady Boyd, *Addicted to Busy* (Colorado Springs, CO: David C Cook, 2014).

> Draw near to God and He will draw near to you
> (James 4:8 NKJV).

1. *Time:* Take actual time to meet with God.
2. *The Bible:* God's Word is the most valuable gift to nurture, grow, and empower your relationship and partnership with Him.
3. *Journaling:* Have conversations with God. Record what you say to Him and what He says to you. God will speak life through the Scriptures as you begin to have practical, *this is the way, now walk in it* conversations.

We must develop the spiritual discipline of meeting with God. It will look different depending on seasons of life. And the reality is that it may look different day by day. I am mindful of times in life when we are dealing with health, family, crises … any number of situations that demand our priority and time. To prepare for those situations, we must build on our daily discipline of spending time with Him.

I found myself leaning into those three—time, Bible, and journaling—as I walked into John 9.

> While walking along the road, Jesus saw a man who was blind (John 9:1a).

Lord,
Why did You just press pause?

I looked up other translations.
And then there it was.
The pause.
The Holy Spirit was hovering over the word *passing.*

Now as Jesus was passing by, he saw … (NET)

Passing by

There is something about the word "passing" that appears so casual, so happenstance, so ordinary—a nothing-extraordinary-planned kind of walking along. Yet as we follow in Jesus' footsteps, we discover there is never anything casual, happenstance, or ordinary about being in the right place at the right time.

And being available.

Jesus was passing by, and He saw. In order for you and me to follow Jesus' example of *seeing,* we cannot pass by Scriptures without giving the Holy Spirit time to speak to us and grow us—to lead us to *see the blind person on the road.*

The next several Scriptures turned into long conversations, lots of digging, and more meditating. They were very directional in terms of *Come, follow Me.*

Lord,
What is it You want to say about passing?
Dear One,
As you walk through these Scriptures, you are becoming an
   astute disciple of Mine. Your prayer "following the life path
   he has cleared" (1 Kings 8:58 MSG) is becoming a compass.
   You are seeing and sensing how the Spirit will direct even
   the most routine day. The closer we walk, as we linger over a
   word or Scripture or picture, I am showing you "This is the
   way; now walk in it."
There was nothing more important for Me to be doing that day.
   Even on the Sabbath I healed.
Your being My representative is a full-time assignment!

Let's talk about ordering your steps.

I was hoping You would.

Take inventory of how you plan. I want you to plan. I want
your steps directed and established by Me. So pray. Ask.
Seek. Knock. I want to breathe Holy Spirit life into your
days, into your brief encounters, into the stresses that cause
angst. I want to bring life where there is sickness and trauma
and even death. I want to open spiritual blind eyes and set
captives free. I want to bring light and truth into where there
is darkness and lies. I want to do this and more, and I want
to do this through you.

Through My Church.

Through My ambassadors.

Though My disciples.

My plan, as we walk through the Gospel of John, is to show
you the way.

> For to this you were called, because Christ also suffered
> for us, leaving us an example, that you should follow His
> steps (1 Peter 2:21 NKJV).

Steps

> The steps of a [good and righteous] man are directed
> *and* established by the Lord,
>   And He delights in his way [and blesses his path]
> (Psalm 37:23 AMP).

Mary,

There is something else I want to make you aware of.

This is weighty.

Don't discount or minimize the impact of even a short encounter with someone. I can do so much with so little. Remember the prayer meeting where you were greeted with a hug. That hug was the domino that caused the walls to fall around your heart. All I need you to do is be you. And you let Me be Me.

Lord, I can do that. I want to do that. I will do that.

Take some time for the Lord to minister to you.

I listened to Tim Sheppard's song, "I Hear the Lord Passing By," and I turned it into a directional prayer for my steps to be ordered by the Lord.

> I hear the Lord passing by
> This could be my day of visitation …
> I wanna see You
> I wanna touch You
> I wanna hold You
> I wanna know You
> I wanna follow You[2]

Come. Follow Me.

Today could be someone's day of visitation because you *passed by.*

It could be yours.

One last linger over the word *passing.* I can't help but exhort each of you, dear readers, to let prayer happen. Naturally.

---

[2] "I Hear the Lord Passing By," words and music by Tim Sheppard © Copyright 2010 Tim Sheppard Music. All rights reserved. Used by permission. In God Be Praised, Gateway Worship, Integrity Music/Gateway Create Publishing, 2010, CD.

Spontaneously. Unexpectedly. Not long, complicated, labor-intensive prayers, but river-of-life praying that flows through you and connects others to God in ways you can't imagine. I receive a daily devotional email, and today's word says it best:

> Don't give up. What needs to have some light shone on it, will have it. It will be the right time and the right place. I will be the One to orchestrate it. You have almost forgotten that this is what you prayed. It wasn't a deep prayer, just one almost in passing, but I heard your heart. I listen at a deeper level than what is evident on the surface. All is good and all is going really well.[3]

Now is the time to let the Holy Spirit speak to you about releasing that river of prayer in you.

Sent

Have you noticed how Jesus notices? How He sees people and situations differently than the world does? Than you and I do?

Lord,
I stood to the side and *watched You* minister to the blind man.
I watched the intentionality, purposefulness, and compassion as You spoke to him.
I stood and watched You minister out of grace, not law.
Pharisees watching, doubters, accusers, and mockers

---

[3] Ras Robinson, "What the Lord is Saying Today." To subscribe to this daily email devotional, go to www.fullnessinchristministries.org.

observing ... but You only had eyes for the blind man. You
could see him, and You wanted him to see You.
And then You sent him to the pool of Siloam.
Mary,
Notice the word Siloam means *sent*.
I was sent by My Father to this blind man. And the blind man
was sent and would testify. And you are sent.
When you are sent, I go with you.
Your steps are ordered by Me.
Let's, you and I, go passing by ...

Has the Lord begun speaking to you about being sent? Is
there something holding you back? Now's the time to get His
perspective, insight, and wisdom about it.
No one wants to just go anywhere.
We always want to be *sent*.

JOHN 10

Hear My Voice

John 10: loved by all who long to hear the voice of God; for those who question if God speaks today and if so, can they discern His voice; for those who are lost and desire to find their way back to Him.

Welcome to John 10.

As a new Christian, finding my way through the unchartered territory of Genesis to Revelation and discovering ways to hear God's voice, I came upon John 10. What wouldn't a new believer love about this chapter? What wouldn't a backslidden or wayward believer love? What wouldn't a seasoned "Follow Me" believer love?

Rhetorical questions, I know. But my pen overflows with gratitude that I have a Savior: Someone who came and rescued me from myself. A Deliverer who came and took all this sin and shame off me and nailed it to the cross. A Shepherd who is with me, helping me navigate this thing called life.

Through the wonders of medicine and technology, I've watched videos capture a deaf person hearing sound for the first time. The emotion that overtakes both the hearer and observers is exhilarating. I am captivated by the looks on their faces as they touch their opened ears and dissolve into rejoicing tears from the miracle of it all.

I have watched firsthand as a man, woman, or child hears the voice of God for the first time—when the spirit is awakened to the heartbeat of God in their spiritual hearing. When the voice of Love becomes louder than the voices of accusation, condemnation, or judgment. When one's spiritual ears are synced to Jesus's voice: *This is one of Mine. Come, follow Me.*

Hearing God's voice is unique to each one of us. It's the same voice but translates differently to every person. Just as humans have love languages, God also has a love language. He speaks to you in the exact manner you are designed to hear. Now hear me on this: the message is the same. God doesn't change. His character and His Word are the same yesterday, today, and forever. But *how* you hear it is what is special to you.

For example, nothing about hunting would speak to me. Nothing. Not the camouflage, not the blind where you sit and wait. … (Well, maybe sitting and waiting would speak to me.) Hunting is just not a language I understand. For others, though, hunting is a language that clearly speaks to them. And it doesn't have to be sitting in a blind. The analogy of hunting and all that goes into being a hunter is full of conversation starters with God.

Math: another language that says nothing to me. Yet I have a friend who loves math. She loves numbers and equations. She loves the $1+1=2$ language. In fact, as my friend was wrestling to hear God about transitions in her life, I asked her what her passion was. "Math," she answered. I replied, "So go there. Expect to hear God speak to you in those terms." And you know what? He did. And she understood.

What's Mary Jo's love language, you may ask? Baking and Challah, but that's another story.

> My sheep *respond as they* hear My voice; I know them *intimately*, and they follow Me (John 10:27).

Jesus says He knows us intimately. How did this happen for

you? Are there still changes you need to make for it to happen? Ask Him. Listen. He is about to give you a plan. Not only is His desire and plan that we know His voice but also that we find our own voice and lend it to giving Him a voice on earth as it is in heaven.

Dearest Lord Jesus,

Today I read a Scripture so dear to me: John 10. Yet because of this ongoing, intentional conversation we are having, it was like reading it for the first time. Sheep. Shepherd. Do You have any idea how grateful I am that You shepherd me? And that You call *Your sheep by name?* And my response is I know Your voice and follow. That's this whole venture in a nutshell: I am Yours, and I follow You. Today I'll linger in my prayer chair, my listening chair, and "be still and hear Your voice."

Those chairs have become your secret place,

safe place,

sanctified place.

Oh the places you have gone from these chairs,

The people you have touched through prayer,

The secrets I have told you.

All in these chairs ... never leaving home. That's one reason I had you name your home Pleasant Place (Psalm 16:5–6).

Isn't it pleasant when we (brethren) dwell together in unity! It is so precious, the anointing oil flows from Me to you in this place (Psalm 133:1–2 MJP).

There are new things on the horizon for you. That's why I need you to be still and know that I am God (Psalm 46:10).

You have learned to hear My voice. Now I want you to find your voice.

Whoa, Lord. That's big!

My intent is for you to echo My voice. I am going to teach
   you how to hear My voice in the middle of your speaking,
   teaching, praying, laughing, walking, writing … I am going to
   teach you to hear My voice as I interrupt your voice and for
   you to speak.
Jesus, I want this, too.

Do you have doubts about hearing God's voice? There is one
main ingredient to hearing it: the Word of God. I cannot say this
loudly enough. Please hear my voice as I shout it from the rooftop:
It's the Word of God! Read it. Meditate on it. Pray it. Ponder it.
Have a conversation with it. The more you have the Word of
God in your heart, renewing your mind and building your spirit
man, the more fine-tuned your hearing the voice of God becomes.

This is one of the reasons I've written this book. Having a
personal conversation with the Father, Son, and Holy Spirit as
you travel through Scriptures will not only bless you from here
to eternity, but it will also do things in your life you couldn't
dream or imagine. When the Word becomes living prayer and
your voice becomes an echo of His voice, heaven takes notice. It
records such agreement, such partnership, such relationship.

Take time now for a heart-to-heart talk with the One who
designed you to hear His voice.

Let's admit it: there are so many voices out there. It's easy to
get caught up, lost, and confused in the airwaves of God's voice,
your voice, and the enemy's voice.

Here is a chart designed by Vicki Porterfield, an international teacher and leader of prayer. Vicki was one of my very

first prayer teachers. This chart will help you discern and judge the voices you hear.[1]

GOD (The Good Shepherd)	SATAN (The Thief)	OURSELVES (The Sheep)
Loves and woos	Drives and forces	Desires attention
Encourages	Intimidates, demands and threatens	Has unreasonable expectations
Gives clear, specific instructions	Exaggerates, gives vague and confusing instructions	Analyzes all instructions
Calls us by name, personal	Uses derogatory, negative speech	Is self-promoting, or self demeaning
Speaks truth, because He values you	Lies, attacks, devalues	Manipulates, controls
Convicts of sin	Blames	Gravitates to painless ways, makes excuses
Speaks in supernatural ways	Uses magic, tricks, spells, sensationalism	Uses reason and logic
Offers hope, strength	Instills fear and doubt	Depends on self, pride
Stretches you	Limits what you can do	Limits you to natural abilities
Doesn't compare you with others	Forces comparison	Compares you to others
Ample provision	Never enough	Is materialistic, self-sufficient
Forgives, offers mercy	Condemns, rejects	Rationalizes behavior
Reconciles	Brings division	Makes excuses, blames others
Transforms	Says things will not change	Works and tries harder
Honors	Brings shame	Covers sin
Wants you to trust God only	Wants you to trust anything but God	Wants you to trust yourself
Wants all the glory!	Wants all the glory!	Wants all the glory!

---

[1] Used by permission. Vicki Porterfield, cofounder of PrayerFields.

How can I walk through these Scriptures without stopping to pray?

Lord, there are so many lost sheep. It breaks my heart.
Mine too!

Many years ago I went to bed nursing a broken heart and crying out to God about prodigals. When I awoke, the Holy Spirit began to speak to me in a poem:

> Mary had her little lambs.
> God said, "They will be your sons and daughters.
> You're to love, teach, and guide them.
> I will lead you in how Mothers oughta's."
>
> There will come a time when each lamb will say,
> "I must go my own way."
> As their mother you will cry inside
> And turn to your Father and pray.
>
> "Please protect and guard them.
> Keep them from world cruel apart."
> And the Father replies, "Do not fear,
> Your Sons and Daughters are Mine.
> I have written their names on My heart."
>
> They may look to the left or the right.
> They may go to the East or the West.
> But the love, joy, and peace I gave to them
> Will prove, by far, to be the best.
>
> When their hearts cry out,
> "Do You love me as I am?"
> I will bring them to Me and say,

"I am Your Shepherd, do not fear.
I love you, and I will show you the way."

So Mother, cry out as you do,
But trust Me as My Word says.
If even one of My lambs may stray and get lost,
I will leave the others, no matter the cost.
I will find My sheep and bring them to Me.
They will know My love and truly be set free.

Is there an end, Lord,
   to prodigals,
      to the heartache,
         to the time lost?
   Is there an end?
Yes, Daughter. What you consider an end will really be their
   beginning.
Let's pray.
Lord, this is just one of the million things I love about You. You
   love prayer as much as I do! There is no better time to talk to
   the Lord about what is lost—people, time, places, resources,

_____.

"But we had to celebrate and be glad, because this brother
of yours was dead and is alive again; he was lost and is
found" (Luke 15:32 NIV).

And to celebrate what is found …

When all the sheep have been gathered, he walks on ahead of them;
   and they follow him because they know his voice (John 10:4).

It's important that we find our voice. God wants to use us
to encourage, exhort, and edify one another. God plans on
using us to pray. Your prayers are unique to you. You represent

a facet of God's heart no one else can. You have found your Shepherd in fields of green pastures, both when you've lost your way and when you've found your way back. God wants to take who He is in you and give that a voice.

In learning to hear His voice, your voice will emerge. Let me pray for you.

> Lord, Your voice draws us to You. Your voice sings over us. Your voice comforts, counsels, teaches, directs, and disciplines us. So much more. Your voice speaks dreams and visions and hope and faith and things that can be and things You want to be. Now give me a voice to echo You. Give me a voice that will break through hindrances and obstacles in others' minds, bodies, and spirits that prevent their hearing you.

JOHN 11

Prodigals

Here we recount the story of Lazarus, Martha, and Mary. Not the whole story, of course. These three appear many places in Scripture, but this particular story is about life and death. About time. About Jesus only doing what the Father tells Him to do. About God being glorified. Are you hearing the theme of John?

We are familiar with this trio, who were more family than friends to Jesus. He came to enjoy the hospitality of Martha, the honor of Mary, and the fellowship of Lazarus. Their home was a place where Jesus was able to rest, refresh, teach, and enjoy His disciples' company. We can glean much from the busyness of Martha, the priorities of Mary, and the death of Lazarus.

Here in John 11, Jesus began a conversation with me. Not about what I had suspected, though. Not about being too busy or the need to draw near or death and miracles.

Rather, about hearts.

Prodigal hearts.

My prodigal heart.

Praying for prodigals' hearts.

Hearts. Yours. Mine. His.

It's often said we can't truly understand others' circumstances and situations—their hurts and pains, their mindsets and hurting hearts—because we have never walked in their shoes. Oh, so true. However, when we allow God to break our hearts for what breaks His, we position ourselves to pray from a place of wisdom, grace, long-suffering, and faith.

Why would one walk away from God and keep walking?

Here we pick up where Jesus left off in John 10:

I love prodigals.
I know You do, Lord.
I was a prodigal. I remember.
I'm glad you remember those days. That's important.
What's the difference, Mary?
   You still have struggles, stresses, sorrow.
   You still fail, get discouraged, and deal with sickness.
   You still wrestle with performance and burn out and being
   overwhelmed.
This is the difference ...

> From the ends of the earth I call to you,
>   I call as my heart grows faint;
>   lead me to the rock that is higher than I
>   (Psalm 61:2 NIV).

As dark as the days were, I was never alone.
   As hopeless as the circumstances seemed, You were there.
      As frustrated or wayward or backward or backslidden ...
      You sought me out.
Your Word gave me hope.
   Your whispers gave me strength.
      Your unfailing love lifted me higher.
Mary,
Don't be surprised that I want to talk about *prodigals.* After all,
   that's why I came to earth—to show the way, bring the truth,
   and give life eternal to those who would believe. I came to do
   the will of the Father. I am to glorify the Father.

I read:

Jesus: His sickness will not end in his death but will bring great glory to God. As these events unfold, the Son of God will be exalted (John 11:4).

Mary, a prodigal is heart-sick. This can be a sickness until eternal death. But I came to rescue, redeem, and restore hearts to the Father. Glory! This brings the Father glory.

Jesus, I love the word *glory.*

Honor.

Praise.

Worship.

Yes … I get it! Your heart is broken for the sick of heart. My heart is too.

Mary, I want to show you a prayer blueprint for prodigals. I want to walk with you through these Scriptures as we pray for lost, lonely, broken, disenfranchised, hurt, hungry souls.

Let's pray.

Lord Jesus, prepare my heart. To see what You see. To hear what You hear. To love how You love. To weep as You weep. To declare as You declare. Life. Life eternal. Amen.

Time. Lord, if I have one regret … Well, I have more than one. But, oh, I wish I had surrendered my life to You sooner than I did. I lost so much time fellowshipping with You. I lost so many opportunities to have You as part of my decision-making. I lost so much and caused myself so much pain. And others. I caused others heartache and pain.

Mary, it's from that place of knowing, of regret, of loss that you can pray for others. As you follow the story of Lazarus being raised from the dead, consider how you can pray for others to hear My voice declare, "Come out."

Lord, that's the blueprint!
Mary, read the Scriptures I spoke:
> Sickness will not end in death (v. 4).

Pray with hope and faith and love.
> Glorify the Father (v. 4).

Pray that the Father is glorified.
> "It is time" (v. 7).

Pray for the timing of God.
> Light versus darkness (vv. 9–10).

Pray for hearts to desire and understand.
> "See *and* believe" (v. 15).

Pray for spiritual eyes to see .
> "Will rise to life" (v. 23).

Pray with faith—this is My will.
> "I am the resurrection and the source of all life" (v. 25).

Pray for a redeeming love to save, heal, deliver.
> Where have they laid his body? (v. 34).

Pray to see their circumstances as I see them.
> "Remove the stone" (v. 39).

Pray for hindrances and hurts to be removed.
> "Come out!" (v. 43).

Pray for the complete work of the Holy Spirit.
> "Untie him, and let him go" (v. 44).

Pray for My victory over Satan's plan to steal, kill, and destroy.
> Glorify the Father (v. 4).

Amen. So be it.
Oh Lord, thank You for reminding me how much You love.
How You love others even more and surely much better than I do. Thank You for shedding new light on this wonderful retelling of Lazarus. I pray ...
Prodigal places in my heart.

Prodigal:
    Idols.
    Dry and thirsty.
    Independent.
    Disheartened.
        Oh, the list can go on and on …

When Bruce and I were first married, we ended each day with a review. How were we doing? Communicating? Any misunderstandings? Words? Actions? Our desire was to keep short accounts. We wanted to ward off any built-up resentments, offenses, and wrongdoings. In fact, this wasn't even our idea. The Bible instructs us not to let the sun go down on our anger (Ephesians 4:26). And this was our desire, too!

Yet life and circumstances, often out of our control or doing, affect our hearts. It is the same with our relationship with the Lord.

Are there any prodigal places in your heart? Areas where you've wandered, worried, or wrecked?

Lord Jesus,
You have always dealt with the interior, inside, hidden heart and the darkness that blinds hearts. These past days I'm digging around in my heart to find hidden judgments, situations, or hurts that hinder my relationship with You and others. There are some that need to be found and uprooted and swept away by the Holy Spirit. I don't want any spiritual darkness in my heart.
I'll take care of you, Mary. Your heart is precious to Me. You gave it to Me so many years ago. You trusted Me. And I have found a *pleasant place* to abide (Psalm 16:6).

Thank You, Lord. So be it, Lord. Thank You, Jesus.

Mary,

Do Me a favor now. Go over this blueprint and apply it to areas in your life where you are struggling.

I know you are a Mary locked in a Martha world.

I know your struggles.

I know your concerns.

I know your heart, and I *dearly* love you (John 11:5).

Mary, I want to remove the stones hindering your moving forward with this _____.

Remember, if you believe, you will see Me glorified in this I have asked of you: _____.

Remember, I declared, "Enough is enough." Today I declare, "Mary, come out! Untie her."

Mary,

If you find My Holy Spirit balance of what Martha and Mary represent, you will stay loosed.

If you weren't so much *Mary*, you wouldn't have so much to give away.

If you weren't so much Martha, you would have given up by now.

You are dearly loved!

How's your heart? There's no better time to take inventory. Don't be in a hurry. A whole, healed heart is God's plan for you. The path may be difficult. It often is a hard-hurting path where we lose our way. Be kind to yourself. In fact, be 1 Corinthians 13:4–7 to yourself as you allow God to get you on the right path again:

Love is patient and kind. Love is not jealous or boastful or proud or rude. It does not demand its own way. It is not irritable, and it keeps no record of being wronged. It does not rejoice about injustice but rejoices whenever the truth wins out. Love never gives up, never loses faith, is always hopeful, and endures through every circumstance (NLT).

Lord, You are the very definition of this Scripture. It's how You love us. I pray for those You have reading this, that their hearts will be touched by You. As they seek You, help them find the answers that truly set them free. The truth of who You are. The truth of how You see them. The truth of how You love them. Amen.

Jesus did not put love in my heart or yours for it simply to stay put. He calls us to love in prayer and then action.

"A new command I give you: Love one another. As I have loved you, so you must love one another" (John 13:34 NIV).

But then, I'm getting a few chapters ahead of myself.

JOHN 12

A heart set on pilgrimage.
Psalm 84:5 NIV

Your Prayer Life

John 12 opens with *Jesus journeyed ...*

What a journey Jesus was on. From the star-filled night in Bethlehem to the town of Bethany on His way to Golgotha, His heart was set on pilgrimage. In the Gospels, Jesus repeatedly tells us, *I have come to glorify the Father, I only do and say what the Father tells Me, and every word I utter originates in Him.* What a relationship!

What Jesus demonstrated day in and day out, at all times and in all places, was living prayer. Prayer is so much more than words. It is worship, thanksgiving, blessing, praise, intercession, asking, petition ... So many expressions of connecting and communicating with God are displayed throughout the Scriptures.

If prayer in its purest form is connecting and communicating with God, then we know it can be wordless. Tears. Listening. Waiting. Hugging. God used a stranger's holy hug to tear down the walls of pain that had kept me from receiving Jesus' love.

Over and over again, Jesus models, mentors, and leads us in living prayer—prayer that involves connecting us to God the Father and connecting others to Him as well.

Constant communion with the Father.

Drawing aside to meet with Him.

Waking early.

Going to the mountain to pray,

Withdrawing to a place of seclusion.

Wherever you are in your prayer life, God wants to take you further. He wants to draw you higher into His heart and deeper into your own.

- Your prayer life evolves, grows, and is nurtured by the Word of God and the Spirit of God. It reflects where we are as a people and what God is saying and doing in the world.
- Your prayer life is an inward expression of your constant communion with the Lord.
- Your prayer life is a response to God's pursuing you.

And then there's worship. Not the worship that requires a gift of music, sounds, voice … All those angelic attributes I'll have to wait until I get to heaven to acquire. But I mean the worship that bows down, that has no other idols before us, that lives a life submitted and committed to glorifying God.

Worship and prayer represent a full circle in the life of a believer.

Where does your prayer end and worship begin?

Where does your worship end and prayer begin?

Worship Is the Key

Before creation, heaven was filled with worship. When God created man, He created prayer. You and I were created to pray. *We were created to pray and worship!*

Take an inventory of how your worship and prayer life interact. Have you kept them separated by function? Let God redefine those boundaries or boxes you may have put worship and prayer in.

People who are marked by encountering God in worship engage Him in prayer.

Worship impacts us. When we turn our affection toward God (Father, Son, and Holy Spirit):

- our hearts change
- our minds change
- the way we see ourselves and others changes
- the way we pray changes

Worship and prayer are foundational expressions of the life flow of every believer.

- Prayer is the expression of our relationship and connection to God.
- Prayer is the language of heaven on earth, in us and through us.
- Prayer is asking, agreeing, thanking, interceding, talking, listening, and waiting.
- As we grow in the Lord, we cannot remove the part of us that is prayer. If we did, there would be nothing left. Prayer is ceaseless. Tireless. Endless.
- Prayer impacts our worship.
- Worship echoes our prayer life.

Speaking of *worship*, we are about to engage with what is, without question, one of the most exorbitant, elaborate, expensive examples of worship in Scripture. You may say, "But Mary Jo, what about Abraham offering Isaac on the altar?" And

I would reply, "You get it." Worship is not just what we do; it is more about *who* we follow and obey.

Bookmark this page. Come back to it often. Allow God to address the worship and prayer in your life.

> To offer your bodies as a living sacrifice, holy and pleasing to God—this is your true and proper worship (Romans 12:1 NIV).

John 12:1 finds us in the home of Martha, Mary, and Lazarus—he "who had recently been raised from the dead" (v. 1). "Formerly deceased Lazarus," verse 9 calls him. Can you imagine the atmosphere at this gathering? Charged with celebration and wonder and gratefulness! And here we see the most wonderful marriage of prayer and worship:

> Mary took a pound of fine ointment, pure nard (which is *both rare and* expensive), and anointed Jesus' feet with it; and then she wiped them with her hair (John 12:3).

Mary. Anointing oil. A life spilled over from prayer to worship.

Not everyone gets it. Not everyone has invested in knowing Jesus. His mission. His purpose. His pilgrimage. Not everyone follows with pure motives. Not everyone has the sensing that Mary did!

Mary,
   So often prayer feels like work, a have-to or a religious exercise. It's none of this.
But I understand. Often, the need is so great it is easy to move your prayer life to a place of desperation. Today I say, "Leave her alone" (John 12:7).
All those "have tos" I want to make "want tos."

All those boxed in, locked in, throw the key away, perfor-
mance-driven prayers, I want to grace with a drawing and a
wooing by My Spirit.

All those how long, how many, how perfectly attached to
prayer—not Me.

You have become a worshipper, a prophetic worshipper, as
you've erased the line between prayer and worship.

Worship is a **key** on this part of our pilgrimage.

I'm on My way to the cross, and I want you with Me. I want
to show you great and mighty things you do not know. I
know, and I'll let you know what you need to know when
you need to know it.

Come, follow Me …

Lord Jesus,

Hindsight is a great gift. It is one of the major bonuses of
getting old! Hindsight. Seeing Your hand and faithfulness
through the years. Being able to look back and finally understand what You were doing despite how it looked or felt at
the time.

I totally understand what Scripture says (John 16) about the
truths not sinking in until You were glorified. We have so
much now.

So much revelation.

So much truth.

So much of the written Word.

So much … the Promise, our Holy Spirit.

Help me steward what You have shown me, where You are
taking me, and what You are calling me to do.

And yes, **worship** will be the **key**!

Love, Mary

Let the Lord know what extravagant worship looks like in your life. And tell Him the impact it has on you. Your heart. Your prayer life. Now is a wonderful time to stop and worship. Let God pour anointing oil onto you.

All that anointing oil, Lord.
I want to pour out on these pages …

John 12:20–28 stops me in my tracks. Men, women, and children, Jews and Greeks—all making the pilgrimage to Jerusalem to worship. It's Passover. Remembering *worship is the key*, Jesus says,

> Anyone who serves Me must follow My path (v. 26a);

Lord, I'm willing to follow You.

> anyone who serves Me will want to be where I am (v. 26b),

Lord, I want to be with You,

> and he will be honored by the Father (v. 26c).

and bring honor to the Father.

Jesus the Human

Now we read Scripture that sheds light on the humanity of our Jesus.

That He experienced everything we do.

That He understands what we are going through and how we wrestle in prayer and have it turn into worship.

Listen as Jesus pours His heart out to Philip and Andrew in verse 27:

- My spirit is low and unsettled (VOICE).
- My soul is in turmoil (ISV).
- My soul is troubled (NIV).
- My soul in greatly distressed (NET).

And Jesus asks,

> What should I say? (ISV)

Lord,
> I can't read these Scriptures without pressing pause. Tears. I get it. This is a wonderful example of You understanding my prayer life. How often I find myself low, unsettled, distressed over people, places, situations, circumstances …
> You understand.

When I say I will follow You, I mean it. There have been times in the past, and I trust there will be times to come, where I will mirror Your prayer:

> How can I ask the Father to save Me from this hour? (v. 27b).

Please give me the strength and the grace to respond in worship like You did.

This hour is the purpose for which I have come *into the world. But what I can say is this:* "Father, glorify Your name!" (vs. 27c–28a).

And then … then … then …. (Oh, how I love Scripture!)

> Suddenly a voice echoed from the heavens.

The Father: I have glorified My name. And again I will bring glory *in this hour that will resound throughout time* (v. 28b).

Lord Jesus, yes! I want to bring glory to my Father and to
have Him bring glory to any and all people, situations, and
circumstances.
Lord, hear my prayer for _____.
Father, be glorified in _____.
Lord,
I am grateful for praying friends. I need them. They need
me. But more than those who stick closer than a brother, I
need to hear from You. I need to settle and hear from You
foremost.

Tentology

Jesus left the people to go to a place of seclusion
(John 12:36b).

Mary,
Face-to-face—My presence. Settle things: situations, circum-
stances, people, pain, anything … nothing is too much for
Me. Meet with Me!
Oh, Lord, there is no place I'd rather be.

I have a favorite word: *tentology*. It's what happens when
you read a Scripture that you've read so many times, but for
some Holy Spirit reason, it's like seeing it for the first time. I'm
talking about Exodus 33:7:

Now Moses used to take a tent and pitch it outside the
camp some distance away, calling it the "tent of meeting."
Anyone inquiring of the Lord would go to the tent of
meeting outside the camp (NIV).

I was drawn to the phrase "tent of meeting," and my spirit resonated with the idea of pitching a tent "outside the camp some distance away." Immediately, the Lord began teaching me the value of cultivating His presence in a place away from the busyness of life. It was the normal practice of Moses to establish a designated place to meet with God.

- "Outside the camp" is established as *separate* from daily life activities.
- It is a place dedicated and consecrated to meet with God.
- It is a place where the presence of God shows up when you do.
- It is a place where the Eternal One talks with you face-to-face.
- It is a place where you meet with God as a friend.

While researching "appointed times" and "divine appointment," I came across the Hebrew word *moed*. I was blown away to see one of its definitions is "tent of meeting." *Of course!* When we pull aside to meet intentionally with God in our appointed place, it is a divine appointment.

Oh, I knew I needed this—a place to meet with God, intentionally removed from distractions, details, and daily to-dos.

The question was "What would this look like in my life?". It was settled. I picked a chair and designated it as my tent of meeting. Here in this chair I would only do one thing: meet with God. I believe the practical application of this Scripture has changed my life—my prayer life and my relationship with the Lord—more than anything else I have done.

Here in this chair, I am "me."

- No one knows me more than Him.
- I don't have to pretend to be braver, stronger, or smarter.

- This is my safe place to be totally transparent and real.
- This is my authentic altar of prayer.

In my prayer chair I'm met with:

- kindness
- wisdom
- mercy
- grace
- forgiveness
- wisdom
- direction
- and so much more!

Over time, this chair became a place of:

- comfort
- counsel
- conversation that flows easily

Over time, this chair became a:

- set apart,
- consecrated,
- and holy place to meet with God.

Over time, this treasured chair became my:

- sanctuary
- shelter
- strong tower
- hiding place

Having cultivated a place to meet with God, I became very aware of His voice and His presence. I found the essence of

my prayer chair was portable. It took up residence in my heart.
I carried within me what transpired or transformed me in
this holy place. I was empowered and equipped to live in the
busyness of life.

Lord Jesus,
   Of all the things You've taught me about prayer, this is the
   example You set in drawing away to meet with God. This
   is such an invitation to a personal, intimate, transparent
   relationship. Of all the things You've mentored, this by far
   has impacted me the most.
Mary,
   This is why.
   This is how.
   This is where.
   This place is the I AM, and from this place, just like Moses,
   My presence will go with you.
Lord, I am cultivating a place to hear Your heart,
   and You are guarding,
      tending,
         watching over my heart.
Dear One.
   When we talked about being sent versus going, the same
   applies to this—your *tent of meeting*.
My tent of meeting!
      It's an affirming place.
      It's a confirming place.
      It's a sending place.
   It's the most adventurous place I've been, Lord.
   Saints, do you have a sanctified, set apart place to meet with
God? My prayer chair has followed me from home to home for

40 years now. This well-loved chair has been re-covered several times, and the cushion gives a little (or a lot); yet when I sit in this chair, it is *home sweet home*.

After one Sunday service, I was praying for people at the altar. This particular Sunday, I met a young mother who had a litany of troubles and concerns. She was overwhelmed. I listened to her. I listened to the Holy Spirit. Then I prayed. I prayed God would show her where to meet with Him. I prayed she would find a place to retreat from the busyness of life and find rest, refreshing, counsel, and wisdom. She told me it would be a miracle, as she lived in a crowded apartment with overstuffed rooms! But I prayed anyway.

A few weeks later she found me at the altar. She was a different person. Her face was lit up, and she was smiling and laughing and couldn't wait to tell me about her *miracle*. The Lord answered our prayers. She found a place to meet with Him: a bathtub! With no water! We rejoiced. Can you imagine how delighted the Father was with her heart and intentionality in meeting with Him?

How about you? Where is your *tent of meeting?*

Look around. Look inward. Look up! We are all so different—different life experiences, families, cultures, religions … The list goes on. Each of us is uniquely created. One of a kind! But each the same in that we were all created to have fellowship with our God.

Here's a poem the Lord gave me about my *tent of meeting:*

> The Same Kind of Different is what you are.
> I searched the earth looking near and far:
> A heart willing to be molded by Me.
> When others look at you it is Me they see.

I called you, I drew you, I sealed you MINE!
Around your heart I drew a boundary line.
Hemmed in by My grace is where I meet you;
That Tent of Meeting to that place you drew.

Face-to-face we meet each and every day.
You sit still, you listen, you hear Me say:
"Beloved, draw nearer," and I speak first.
My Presence, My voice, your heart immersed.
It is this place where you abide—
Me in you, you in Me, Bridegroom, Bride.
Where is your tent, this is where we start,
A chair, a closet, a blanket set apart.

Sanctified from this place, the desire to be
My glory resting on you, you'll be set free.
Submitted, committed, permitted you'll go.
Refreshed, renewed, restored My spirit will flow.

This Tent of Meeting will become portable
As My spirit is with you wherever you go.
In the busyness of each day's demands,
You'll stop, draw in, your life in My hands.

As Moses discovered and My Son displayed,
It's the Tent of Meeting where they prayed.
It's this special place transformed to be
The Same Kind of Different as Me.

JOHN 13

We've arrived at chapter 13. Pull up a chair. For the next five chapters, we are going to participate in what is known as the Last Supper. Not spectating. Not reading about. Rather, *being* part of the dialogue, the beautiful prayer monologue, and then … the Garden. That's right. Almost 25% of the Gospel of John is in the Upper Room—Jesus and His 12 disciples. And today, you and me.

Servant Leader

You may be surprised to learn that one of the things I love most about prayer is the juxtaposition of being known by God and being nameless and faceless with others. Let me explain.

There is no one who knows me better than I know myself than God. There is no one I can be more honest and transparent with. There is no safer place to be loved, disciplined, and discipled than by the Holy Spirit through the Word (Jesus) to live the will of God. The intimacy of this relationship is real and raw and authentic.

In this private place, God works on your heart, much like the clay on a potter's wheel. In this place, broken pieces are put back together again—stronger and better, with no evidence of the break. From this place, worship and prayer begin to overflow and touch every facet of your life. The wonder of prayer and praying!

In this place you learn John 13. In this place you are humbled, and Jesus comes and washes your feet, so often dirty with sin, soiled with unforgiveness, and bleeding from offenses. In this place, you humble yourself before our mighty God and submit to the wonder of Jesus washing your feet.

Servant.

Leader.

Then from this place, you pray. And God tells you secrets. And you pray in secret. And you serve God and others through agreeing in prayer. The most powerful prayer you can pray is, "Father, how do You want me to pray?" From this place of submitting your will, what you think is best, and what you may want to pray, God begins to give you His burden. His perspective. His will for the person, situation, city, country, nation, etc. And you pray. And you "wash the feet" of the one you are praying for. And you fight for the will of God to be executed on earth as it is in heaven.

Servant.

Leader.

I currently serve as a pastor in the prayer and prophetic department of my church. When I joined the staff, my first task was to begin developing a culture of prayer and intercession with a focus on praying for the church's leadership as well as countless other prayer needs.

I had the privilege and honor of developing leadership teams. One area of team development that was of the utmost importance was the character of the intercessors. The enemy would like nothing better than to introduce kryptonite to our passion and the purity of our hearts in serving God and serving others. This kryptonite is pride: having to attach your name or a *God told me so* to answered or unanswered prayers. Nameless, faceless praying is serving God and others without seeking position or power. It does not manipulate people or situations. In this place of serving others, the only agenda is God's. Staying in the place of Jesus washing our feet so we can, through prayer, wash others' feet is the most powerful praying position an intercessor can be in. It all starts here!

Servant.

Leader.

> "And since I, your Lord and Teacher, have washed your
> feet, you ought to wash each other's feet"
> (John 13:14 NLT).

Have you ever participated in a foot washing? When led by the Spirit, it can be a very powerful representation of Jesus' ministry. I've seen foot washings done at weddings and by leaders for significant passages of ministry. I've even done a few myself, and I can tell you this: it's always harder to be on the receiving end. It is very humbling.

As I gathered my new leadership team together, we prayed and launched this intentional ministry of serving our leadership and others through prayer and intercession as God spoke to us. One of the male leaders (Rob) felt impressed to repent on behalf of men who have abdicated their place in praying to women. I also felt impressed to follow in prayer and repent on behalf of women who have reserved and preserved prayer and not left a place for men.

We followed with a foot washing. I washed Rob's feet and prayed for the men of our church to rightfully take their place as leaders, fathers, and men. Rob washed my feet and prayed for the women to feel the partnership and strength of us all coming together in prayer. Hindsight has shown the power of that moment—faithful, faith-filled men and women, nameless

and faceless, serving every department and every prayer request.
Every event saturated in men and women praying.

Jesus,
Here I am, leaning into the Word as John the Beloved did.
So aware of what is coming, and this last will and testament,
so to speak, is weighty. Every word. Every action.
Lord,
Do You have any idea how hard this is? I know just how
Peter felt. I want to be washing Your feet.
Beloved,
Through all the days and in all the ways I have walked with
you,
Through the signs and wonders and miracles,
Through the times and uprisings with religious systems—
I only do what the Father tells Me to do, Mary.
I will wash your feet.

If I don't wash you, you will have nothing to do with Me (John 13:8).

Come, follow Me.
Jesus, yes. Even in this, I will follow You.

Something supernatural happens when we submit to what
seems unnatural or out of order. Jesus, help me understand.
Help me receive.

Love and faithfulness meet together;
righteousness and peace kiss each other
(Psalm 85:10 NIV).

And then from John to Peter to …

Jesus,

Sometimes I feel like Judas. It's a horrible feeling. Betrayal.
Unfaithful. Disloyal.
Why do I shrink back from bold witnessing?
Why do I fear man?
Why do I question Your promptings?

Mary,

NO! Your heart has never been cold toward Me. Your love
and devotion have never been in question. But two things I
want to say:
One, those are good questions but not the right analogy.
Two, there are those who will betray me. They will sell out
for what the world has to offer. Their hearts will grow cold.

"And because lawlessness will be increased, the love of
many will grow cold" (Matthew 24:12 ESV).

Mary, I want you to pray. I need you to pray. Others need you
to pray. Pray. Believe. Hearts grow cold.

Jesus, sometimes I feel like Peter. Confident and boldly
proclaiming I would give my life to You and then denial ...
denying the very One I chose to follow.

Mary,

Now is the right time to ask those earlier questions.
Moving forward with confidence. Mary, be you! Be bold
when I ask you to be bold. Witness with words when I ask
you to. Be courageous when I lead you to battle. Do not go
into battle ahead of Me. Go with Me. Be brave when sent. I'll
be with you.

I know, Lord, when You see me, You see a Joshua.

When I see me, I hear a Christopher Robin speaking to Winnie
the Pooh!

If ever there's a tomorrow when we're not together, there's something you must remember.... You're braver than you believe and stronger than you seem and smarter than you think. But the most important thing is even if we're apart, I'll always be with you.[1]

I love You, Lord.
I love you too, Mary.

⸾

I trust you are having your own conversation with Jesus. Yours may sound very different from mine. Or perhaps we wrestle with the same heart condition. Whatever the case, this is one of the most important meals you will have with Jesus. In fact, the next one is the last chapter on the shores of Galilee. There is much road to travel between now and then. Take time. Recline at the Savior's chest, submit to His Word, and ask your questions. Leave this meal prepared in greater measure to walk the way to the cross with Him.

---

[1] Karl Geurs, dir. *Pooh's Grand Adventure: The Search for Christopher Robin.* 1997; USA: Walt Disney Home Entertainment, 2006, DVD.

JOHN 14

The End and the Beginning

Imagine with me: Jesus has surrounded Himself with His most faithful friends, trusted disciples, and soon-to-be voices and heart of His life's message to the world. Imagine the weightiness of the words being spoken. This is going to be a Passover feast like no other.

In this sobering moment the apostles hear their Teacher's last lingering conversation. Jesus takes this time to reinforce His mission and what He was entrusted to do in these men. Every word is rich with meaning, and the message lives on for you and me today. The disciples may not have been fully aware of the pending events, but Jesus was.

I'm familiar with death. I'm well acquainted with the grief and sadness and longing attached to it. I know there is no good time or good way to lose a loved one. A quick death leaves no time for earthly goodbyes. So many things left unsaid leaves one wishing for one more word, one more laugh, one more story, one more tear, one more phone call, one more visit … Lord, just one more. A slow death, often met with sickness or disease, creates pain and heartache in not being able to really help. Young: a life cut short. Old (by biblical standards): wrapped in memories that are very much alive and part of who we are.

I've had the privilege of being at the bedside when a last breath was drawn. I've had the honor of being witness to heaven touching earth in an indescribable way. I've had the joy of knowing with confidence that the loved one is experiencing the fullness of Psalm 17:15:

> When I awake, I will see you face to face and be satisfied (NLT).

Earthly goodbyes are so hard. I remember last words—emotions evoked with bedside waiting, the unexpected, and then the inevitable goodbye. Death feels so final. Yet it truly represents a beginning, not an end.

These experiences make John 14 so dear, so real, and so promising. Here Jesus gives us an eternal perspective of what is to come after this earthly body.

Lord,
> I know You say, "Don't despair."
> I know there's that balance of
>> loving life but not holding on too tightly and
>> not fearing death but not wanting to let go.

Dearly Beloved,
> We are gathered here ...
> A familiar refrain at the beginning of weddings. Marriages. The coming together of bride and groom. The miracle of 1+1=1. Unity. Covenant.
> Are you surprised that I would talk marriage while you're speaking of death?

Well, You are right, Lord. I surely didn't expect to hear a *Here comes the Bride,* but now that You mention it ...

I want you to know this is the kind of celebration awaiting each of My beloved disciples. All those who have called upon My name, believed in God, and believed in Me.

"I will be there to greet you personally." (John 14:3).

Dear Jesus,
Please stop for a minute! Your love feels so real right now. It's overwhelming. I just want to sit in Your presence and by the Spirit rest in this moment.

Dear ones, take a moment. Just for yourself.

Lay aside any grief, loss, confusion, pain, hurt, longing. Put all that aside for a moment and allow the Holy Spirit to speak to you about you. Let Him give you an eternal perspective of where your journey will lead you. Permit the Spirit to deposit in you a holy longing for heaven yet a passionate fervor for the days at hand and ahead.

And allow the Holy Spirit, the Comforter, to grieve with you for premature earthly goodbyes, to unanswered prayers, to conversations not finished, to words not said. He's so good at comforting the brokenhearted. And remember:

> "Blessed are those who mourn,
>   for they will be comforted" (Matthew 5:4 NIV).

Mary,
I want to talk about prayer.
Oh, Lord, me too!
Jesus, I can get so lost in John 13–17. Not lost as in not finding my way but lost as in caught up in the enormity of what You are saying.
I'll be a student of prayer the rest of my life.
The more I learn or understand about prayer, the more
I realize I don't know and how much *more* there is to comprehend.

When one word represents the expression of our relationship
on earth …
When one word gives height and depth and width and
breadth to communion with You, and the Father and the
Holy Spirit …
When one word speaks to the affection You have for me and
mine for You …
When one word gives expression to the fullness of why You
created me …

I get so lost.

I want to learn more.

I want to be growing in prayer the rest of my life.

I want my prayer life to be more than it was yesterday and less
than it will be tomorrow.

Mary,

Contained in this chapter are the keys to your prayer life:
Abide.
Ask.
Holy Spirit.

These three **keys** will continue giving you unbridled **joy** in
prayer until we do meet face-to-face.
Abide.
Ask.
Holy Spirit.

Jesus,

Remember that night? The night when my *beginning* began.
The night I surrendered my messed-up life to You. The night
the Promise of the Holy Spirit filled me to overflowing.
That night, I first heard the whisper that became an anchor,
a compass, a light-to-my-path.
I am in you. You are in Me.

When I read those words this morning, they still resonate deeply in my spirit. As clear to me as the night I first heard them.
I am in you. You are in Me.
You were speaking so clearly.
 This is what our relationship will look like. This is how it will work. This is the key to prayer—
  effective,
   joyful,
    powerful,
     meaningful!
Prayer is rooted,
 nurtured,
 matured
 through abiding!

Abide

"I am in you. You are in Me. Abide."

I didn't know it then. It was months later when I stumbled across John 14 and 15. There was *abide!* And Jesus began teaching me what the word *abide* actually means and what abiding in Him means to my prayer life.

I did a Scripture word search for *abide:*

1. Let the Word of God abide, dwell, inhabit in me (Colossians 3:16).
2. Lord, who may abide, dwell, sojourn, get invited, take refuge in Your tabernacle? (Psalm 15:1).
3. Those who trust, lean on, confidently hope in the Lord … abide forever (Psalm 125:1).

The Lord was instructing me that the way I would learn to pray was the Word of God, cultivating a heart for Him to take up residence and trusting in Him completely.

Lord,
It hasn't been a smooth road. I've taken You on a pretty bumpy ride through my decisions, detours, and dead ends. But You, ever the faithful. Always calling me back and calling me higher. Prayer has paved the way. Prayer has made the way. Prayer has kept the way to abiding in You.
Mary,
When I see *abide* I think *bride*.
Your walk down the aisle is a beautiful one.
Thank you for taking the keys I have given you and using them to unlock doors for others.

How lovely are the feet of her who brings good news (Isaiah 52:7 MJP).

What does *abide* look like in your life? Doing a Scripture word study will open revelations for how Jesus and you are one in the Father.

Ask

One night, surrounded by family and friends, I prayed the sinner's prayer. That's right. I was a sinner—so separated from the will of God, the heart of God, and the ways of God. Brokenhearted I was. But I asked. And do you know what I asked for? I asked for peace. My life was turned upside down and inside out. My buried pain could no longer stay hidden. I was living a pretend life for everyone else to see, but the One who was pursuing me knew all. I couldn't hide from Him. So I asked for peace. And peace I received. Peace that sustained me through the coming days, weeks, and months as my unraveled life began healing. Peace that held me as I whispered a last "I love you" as my mother slipped into heaven. Peace that strengthened me when the invitation to *Follow Me* cost more than I had emotionally. Peace.

And what did I learn that was so key to my prayer life? I *needed* to ask. I found I did not have because I did not ask (James 4:2). My prayer life could not and would not be one of presumption. I use the word "presumption" because the Word is filled with promises of God, but I would not presume on Him. My relationship with the Father, Jesus, and the Holy Spirit was rooted in my *asking*. I wanted (and He did too) a relationship in which I was dependent on Him. Ask. Knock. Seek. And I did.

Mary,
The real key to asking is the works that I do, he will do also; and greater works than these he will do (John 14:12). When you ask in My name, you are asking for greater works that I may be glorified. I want you to ask for your needs and wants and desires … for you and others. But Mary, "in My name" is for the greater works that will glorify the Father.
Oh Lord, I love that! I get it!
Knowing full well, You are aligning my asking with Your greater works. Order my steps. In Jesus' name, I pray.

> Aware of how literally
> I don't stop and ask.
> I go about my busy day

from task to task.
Ordering my steps?

I can't really say!
Each hour, each moment
slipping away
While Father waits
for me to pray.
How? Where? What? When?
Your plans for me today?
Reminded afresh simply
Ask. He'll tell me the way.

Is asking hard for you? Is it easier to ask for other people than yourself? Is asking hindered by unanswered or delayed prayers? Take inventory and *ask*.

Holy Spirit

I'm grateful I was raised knowing God: Father, Son, and Holy Spirit. Yes, I did get to know the Trinity through my family's faith, through my parochial teaching, through my religious disciplines. And I'm grateful. There was never a question—no matter how far I strayed, how dark my life became, or how lost this sheep was—about the truth, reality, and constant of the one true living God.

But that night (March 16, 1976), I stepped over the line drawn around my heart that was religion and stepped right into the loving arms of Jesus and met the Holy Spirit. How grateful I am that my relationship with Jesus always, from day one, included the Helper, the Holy Spirit.

And help He did. He took my prayers seriously!

Jesus,

I can't imagine my prayer life without the help of the Holy Spirit.
It's as if, sitting here, my life with You is passing before me,
and the thread holding it together is the Holy Spirit.

Mary,

As much of a mystery that has kept theologians busy for
thousands of years … It's less of a mystery and more of a
miracle when you pray Father, Son, Holy Spirit. Separate
but one.

The time you have spent getting to know the Helper has
kept your prayer life powerful, effective, and, honestly,
surprising and awing you much of the time. The Holy
Spirit is like that.

Taking time to get to know the third person of the Trinity
will empower your prayer life like nothing else. The very
first Bible study program I led was centered on *The Helper*
by Catherine Marshall. There are so many wonderful
books written about the Holy Spirit and how to know Him
personally.

Want help with your prayer life? Get to know the
Holy Spirit. His fruit (Galatians 5:22–23). His gifts
(1 Corinthians 12; Romans 12). And so much more!

The Holy Spirit:

- Teaches (John 14:26)
- Points to truth (John 15:26)
- Leads (Romans 8:14)
- Speaks (1 Corinthians 2:13)
- Guides (John 16:13)
- Gives life (Genesis 6:3)

- Prompts (Acts 8:29)
- Intercedes (Romans 8:26)
- Uncovers sin (John 16:8)

Lord,

You used a word that has taken on more importance to me as of
late:

Legacy

To give

It's given me a lot to think about. I've enjoyed years. There has
never been a birthday that I struggled with the number. Life
is such a gift. I've outlived both parents and said an earthly
goodbye to two sisters. I am very mindful of days and weeks
that disappear into months and years. I do not live with an
Ecclesiastes 1:2–4 mentality:

> "Everything is meaningless," says the Teacher, "com-
> pletely meaningless!"
>
> What do people get for all their hard work under the
> sun? Generations come and generations go, but the earth
> never changes (NLT).

I believe in leaving a legacy—

a spiritual legacy.

I believe in counting my days and praying that they count.

Dear Mary,

That is the gift of prayer. Prayers do not die. Intercession
lives on.

These chapters are filled with My prayers. *And you are
an answer to these prayers. The Church is an answer to these
prayers. Prayers are the legacy I have invested in you.*

Oh, Lord, I pray so. I know so. Thank You!

You know what Jesus says He leaves us as His legacy? Peace.

Jesus: My peace is the legacy I leave to you. I don't give gifts like those of this world. Do not let your heart be troubled or fearful (John 14:27).

As Jesus faced the ultimate test of "Your will be done," He spoke of peace—that peace that passes understanding and the world does not know. How is your peace-ometer? Friends, anchor yourself in these verses until Jesus gives you that peace. It's your inheritance. It's your DNA. It's who you are because it's who He is.

JOHN 15

As I read and meditated on the powerful chapters of John 13–17, I felt a sonnet break out of me. If I could pen words like Elizabeth Barrett Browning to her beloved Robert, this is the song I would sing to my Lord:

> How do I love thee? Let me count the ways.
> I love thee to the depth and breadth and height
> My soul can reach, when feeling out of sight
> For the ends of being and ideal grace.
> I love thee to the level of every day's
> Most quiet need, by sun and candle-light.
> I love thee freely, as men strive for right.[1]

The gravity of this moment. The enormity of what is about to happen. The ultimate clash of light and darkness, truth and lies.

Keeper

I grew up hearing these phrases: "She's a keeper." "He's a keeper." "That's a keeper." They imply an affection, desire, or conclusion about something precious. And when I read the Father is the keeper of the vineyard, I feel very watched over, taken care of, included … very covered with attention and intentionality.

---

[1] Elizabeth Barrett Browning, "How Do I Love Thee?" (Sonnet 43), lines 1–7.

Father: Keeper of the vineyard.
    Settled.
Jesus: The Vine.
    Secure.
Me: The branch.
    Satisfied.

Jesus,
There's something so comforting about being part of the
    vineyard, vine, and branch.
    But then there's the *pruning* …
This showed up in my email today, Lord:

> You are at a point where you cannot move ahead
> without getting rid of stuff from the past. There are
> issues that have been painful and out of your ability to
> control or do anything about except to leave them
> behind. You cannot make significant progress until
> you look forward and refuse to allow those things to
> bog you down, says the Lord. Philippians 3:13:
> Brethren, I do not count myself to have apprehended;
> but one thing I do, forgetting those things which are
> behind and reaching forward to those things which are
> ahead [NKJV].[2]

So this is why *abiding* had been difficult as of late.
This is why I felt weighed down.
This is why my prayers were locked up in my heart or on the
pages of my Bible, and my mind wandered.

---

[2] Used by permission. Marsha Burns, "July 13, 2017," Small Straws In A Soft
Wind, July 13, 2017, accessed January 18, 2018, https://ft111.com/straws23.htm#-
JULY_2017.

Mary,

There's more to learn about *abide*.

I know, Lord.

   I agree. If seeing You means we have seen the Father,
   doesn't it make sense that as I abide in You, others will see
   You, understand the Father, and become aware of the Holy
   Spirit?

   Doesn't that make sense?

   I mean, Lord, I do want my life to become so transparent,
   that thin veil, so others see right past me and see You!

Beloved, that desire you have is the work of the Spirit. This is
   the part of *abide* I want you to grab hold of, understand, and
   begin living.

   There is something more about *abiding* I want you to get. Yes,
   I want others to see Us when they see you, but I also want
   you to see the Father, Jesus, and Holy Spirit when you see
   you! You know when you let what other people say and do
   bother you? When you stew and fret and have those mind
   conversations with and about them?

   That is *not* abiding.

Ouch! Lord, You are right. I get what You are saying. Point
   taken. Thank You!

I am not bothered by repetitive messages in Scripture. On
the contrary, these are core truths Jesus goes to great lengths
to make certain we hear. Remember, "faith *comes* by hearing,
and hearing by the word of God" (Romans 10:17 NKJV).
Abiding.

Linger or return to *abiding* often. Check your roots. Check
your fruit. Check the pruning.

Friend

There it is, Lord:

> Follow My example (John 15:10).

I know this is the root of abiding. Thank You for coming to show the way and be the truth and the life!

> Love one another as I have loved you (John 15:12 NKJV).

Lord, this is easy to read, memorize, and quote. But oh, Lord, the kind of love You have shown … and I know we are chapters away from the cross … that kind of love, Lord, requires more than what I naturally have.

I attended a wedding where the officiating pastor used 1 Corinthians 13 ("The Love Chapter") for the couple's vows. The Lord reminded me of those as I pondered the love He was calling out of me.

> I promise that I will be patient with you.
> Be kind to you and not envious or boastfully proud.
> I will not be selfish or rude toward you
> And will choose not to be easily angered.
> I will not keep a record of the things you've done wrong.
> I will not delight in evil but will rejoice in the truth.
> I will always protect you, always trust you, always hope the best for you,
> And always preserve together with you, in unconditional love …

Mary,

This love is the love We put in your heart … for others … and
for yourself.

And, Mary, that's why I will send the Helper.

You're right, Lord.

And Mary, you have laid down your life for Me.

You have loved when you've been hurt.

You have loved when misunderstood, mocked, abandoned.

You have the Helper.

Hold tight … We have more to do, more to love, more to help,
more …

I want more, Lord.

That's why I call you Friend.

I was surprised and blessed beyond measure with the gener-
osity of Jesus' words to me. Often, I examine and measure my
fruit from a perspective of "there is so much more." That day
the Lord wanted me to see from His perspective, and it filled
me with grace, kindness, and love!

And He called me *Friend.*

Friendships can be a funny thing … or not so funny. We now
live in a world of virtual friendships through social media—
checking Facebook to see how many friends I have, how many
friends so-and-so has, constant posts … We all have a history
of friendships from childhood to those painful teenage years
and then to adulthood where we learn which relationships are
"friends who stick closer than a brother" kind of friends. Those
for better or worse.

That's why it caught me off guard when I first heard Jesus
call me Friend. *Friend.* Jesus wants to be my friend. I know
Scripture says Jesus calls me friend (John 15:15). He also tells us

that the Holy Spirit is going to be our friend. So here we have Father God, Jesus, and the Holy Spirit wanting to be my friend. How does that translate to my prayer life? Easy. Well, not so easy for some of us …

> "I'm telling you these things while I'm still living with you. The Friend, the Holy Spirit whom the Father will send at my request, will make everything plain to you. He will remind you of all the things I have told you. I'm leaving you well and whole. That's my parting gift to you. Peace. I don't leave you the way you're used to being left—feeling abandoned, bereft. So don't be upset. Don't be distraught" (John 14:26–27 MSG).

> But the Father will send the Friend in my name to help you. The Friend is the Holy Spirit. He will teach you all things. He will remind you of everything I have said to you (John 14:26 NIRV).

There was a time when I was deeply wounded by a friend. I know, and you'll agree, friends are an investment of time, heart, transparency, vulnerability, and truth. When this friendship ended, I made an inner vow: "I will never have another best friend." God heard me.

Weeks later, I was sitting in church and so happened to be sitting next to a casual acquaintance. I heard the Lord whisper, "Let her love you." What? No! Didn't God hear what I had determined? No more best friends. But instead, I repented for the inner vow I had made, trusted God's voice, and obeyed His request to "let her love you." The result? Friends. Best friends. What a gift from God.

And now we have Jesus calling us *Friend*. This is a whole different level of relationship.

Living Prayer

to

Abide

is to

pray
without ceazing

"Abide in Me
& I in you." JOHN 15:4

Prayer
is not something I do.

Prayer
is who I am.

I will be a student of prayer all of my life.

Jesus, what an invitation!

Come

A personal
hand-in-hand
Emmaus Road

that VOICE

DEEP CALLING TO DEEP PSALM 42:7

Follow
Me

Yes, Lord

walk through the
scriptures of John
at the pace & rhythm
of Holy Spirit

Goodness & Mercy
shall follow me

I call you Friend.

It does Jesus a disservice, and you as well, to measure your friendship with Him based on earthly friendships. Even the best of the best of the best friends. With Jesus, there is more. It's like that song, "What a Friend We Have in Jesus."

I've heard some people say they don't have a best friend. I want to introduce them to my Jesus.

JOHN 16

Avoid the Offenses

Dearest Lord Jesus,

Before I start John 16, I just want to say what pure joy this devotional and time with You has been. I can't express enough how full my heart is and how devoted and grateful I am. I pray my life surrendered is an expression of my sincere gratitude, thanksgiving, and praise.

I can't imagine doing life without the Helper. He has revealed and uncovered sin in my life. Do You remember when newly saved—a babe in faith—and praying, I said to You, "I don't think I have sin in my life. Please show me!"? And He did! And He continues to speak and uncover and heal and restore me. How grateful I am.

Mary,

I trust these words further answer your questions how We are one:

> Father,
>
> Son,
>
> Holy Spirit.
>
> Three in One; fullness, functioning, faith in, for, and through you!

There are some conversations that don't need dialogue. Don't need questions. Don't need responses. There are some conversations where you just want to listen. And pray. And absorb. And receive revelation. John 16 is one of those chapters.

I put myself in the apostles' place—all they'd heard, seen, witnessed, and lived walking with Jesus the past three years. Now this. So much of chapter 16 is summarizing. Giving them their marching orders. Setting a footprint in front of them so they know how to move forward. Without Him. But not alone. *Follow Me.*

This chapter is full of Father, Son, and Holy Spirit. These verses unfold a relationship that will keep us.

Keep us connected.

Keep us focused.

Keep us dedicated.

Read John 16 in its entirety. Slowly. Pause. Take it in. It may sound similar to chapter 15 and other conversations Jesus had with His disciples. But this chapter has a resonance, a weightiness, all its own. It's Jesus' last words of counsel and comfort before He begins to pray to the Father for you and me. Walk with me through these verses.

Jesus: I am telling you all of this so that you may avoid the offenses that are coming" (John 16:1).

Lord,

I want to be bold and strong and courageous like Joshua. I want to proclaim and live my faith out loud. I am not ashamed of the gospel of Jesus Christ. But Lord, I hear You say:

Pick your battles.

And when you pick your battles, choose your weapons.

And when you choose your weapons, know how to use them.

And when you use them, be led by the Spirit.

For *when* is as important as *how* is as important as *who* is as important as *what* is as important as *where,* and I am the *why*!

Lord, forgive me for the times I've shrunk back, ran away,
 was taken out by ear of man, was intimidated, and didn't
 represent.
Mary,
You are one of My sheep, and I am sending you out in the midst
 of wolves. I need you to be wise as a serpent and harmless as
 a dove (Matthew 10:16). Always be true to who you are. In
 Christ. Settle it now. You will be misunderstood, mocked,
 betrayed, dismissed, persecuted … Offenses are coming.
 Be led by the Spirit.
     Speak without words.
     Speak with actions.
         Speak boldly.
         Speak humbly.
             Speak with love.
             Speak with truth.
Yes, my Lord.

This is truly a *You must increase, and I must decrease* living.
Persecution, Not being accepted. Being mocked or misrepre-
sented and often discriminated against because of my faith.
     Lord, help me.
         Help me respond.
         Help me process.
         Help me represent.

And Mary, avoid the offenses.

I knew the word *avoid* meant to keep away from, steer clear
of, and refrain. I looked up the word *offenses*, and I asked the
Holy Spirit to put that word under the microscope for me.

Offend:
- Stumbling block
- Entice to sin
- Cause a person to begin to distrust or desert one whom he ought to trust and obey
- Cause to fall away

Lord,

I'd like to think I am not easily offended.

I do a lot of filtering and give a lot of grace, but there is an increased leaning toward taking up an offense. The political climate can bring all sorts of attitudes and judgments up. Social media gives us access to strangers' lives and much of it reflecting a culture going awry. Situations and circumstances out of our control have a way of causing ire to rise up.

Mary,

All that you say is true.

But what I spoke to the apostles as we gathered at the Passover meal is as true today as it was then. *Avoid offenses.* Stay on course. Seek Me first.

These distractions can and will become stumbling blocks.

There's so much I need and want you to do, say, love, pray…

Mary, avoid offenses.

You are so right, Lord.

You are letting little things bother you. You begin to rehearse mental conversations. You spend time stewing. You engage in conversations through social media posts and other people's exchanges, and you get off track. I call these little foxes that can become roaring lions that seek to kill, steal, and destroy.

The Man
> Get up, my dear friend,
>> fair and beautiful lover—come to me!
> Let me see your face,
>> let me hear your voice.
> For your voice is soothing
>> and your face is ravishing.

The Woman
> Then you must protect me from the foxes,
>> foxes on the prowl,
> Foxes who would like nothing better
>> than to get into our flowering garden
>> (Song of Solomon 2:10, 14–15 MSG).

I created you to pray. I will let you know your battles. And then I will go before you. I will never send you into a battle unprotected. Unprepared. Ill-equipped. Follow Me.

Oh Lord, You are so right. I commit to guard my eyes, ears, and heart. And follow You!

I love the Holy Spirit's microscope. Take some time and let the Lord minister to those areas of offense and the traps that ensnare you into carrying an offense.

The Helper

Jesus took such great care to forewarn me about the pitfalls of living prayer out loud. How about you? How are you weathering these present day shifts in culture, church, and government? You know it will always be changing. That's why I'm not putting a year on this. Fifty years from now there will always be pressures from the outside. Our position must be clear. We do not conform to the world. We do not cave to peer pressures. We do not change the Word to adapt to current events. Yes, we will always be swimming upstream—being the light and love and salt Jesus called us to be.

Remember when Peter wanted to build a tent for Jesus, Moses, and Elijah in Luke 9? We're often like that—we want to keep things status quo. Hold onto what we know. But Jesus knows better. In John 16, He makes it clear: He has to go so the Helper can come. It's one thing for you and me to look at these Scriptures and understand what Jesus means. But what faith must have been activated in that room for the disciples even to consider it a good thing for Jesus to leave. After all, He just called them *friend*!

How can you pick one favorite name for the Holy Spirit? Woven throughout the Scriptures from "In the beginning" (Genesis 1:1) to "Amen" (Revelation 22:21), the Holy Spirit partners with God the Father and the Son on our behalf. He is characterized in many different ways, such as wind, fire, seal, water, oil, and dove.

The Holy Spirit is the:

- Spirit of Truth (John 14:16–17)
- Spirit of Holiness (Romans 1:4)
- Spirit of Life (Romans 8:2)
- Spirit of Adoption (Romans 8:15)
- Spirit of Grace (Hebrews 10:29)
- Spirit of Glory (1 Peter 4:14)
- Eternal Spirit (Hebrews 9:14)

Some may say, "But what does He *do*?" Oh, I'm so glad you asked!

- He convicts us of sin.
- He prepares our hearts to receive Jesus.
- He comforts us.
- He counsels us.
- He advocates for us.
- He abides with us.
- He guides us into truth.
- He makes intercession for us.
- ... and more!

Consider all the Holy Spirit wants to do in and through your life. Recall the times when He was your comforter, counselor, and guide. Are there ways you can lean in more to this special relationship? Are there ways you've limited the power of the Holy Spirit in your life?

Now's a good time to talk to Him about just this.

Persistent Prayer

I love Scriptures that speak to the relationship of the Father, Son, and Holy Spirit and how I should pray.

> The Spirit of truth will come and guide you in all truth. He will not speak His own words to you; He will speak what He hears, revealing to you the things to come and bringing glory to Me. The Spirit has unlimited access to Me, to all that I possess and know, just as everything the Father has is Mine. That is the reason I am confident He will care for My own and reveal the path to you (John 16:13–15).

To pray the will of the Father.

To pray the Word of God, which is Jesus.

To pray for the works (power) of the Spirit of God.

I was raised to pray rote prayers. They were beautiful. But I never expected an answer or response to them. Now, I did pray asking prayers. But honestly, they were never conversational. They didn't involve listening or dialogue. More monologue, really—prayers from my needs and some wants. Never spoken with the thought that when the prayers went up, they would be heard and answered by a loving God.

As a new believer, I sat under Spirit-filled, Word teaching. I learned to understand the Word, pray the Word, be hungry for the Word, embrace the Word ... to *live* the Word. I cultivated the Holy Spirit in me. I practiced praying in the Spirit—a syllable, a word, a sentence, a phrase, a language, and a conversation. I exercised my spiritual muscles.

Now, I often pray in the Spirit before I read the Word. I ask the Lord to speak to me and give me a Scripture, and because I am His sheep and I hear His voice, I believe He will. And my Spirit is quickened by the Word.

How does your prayer life reflect your relationship with ...

- The Father?
- The Son?
- The Holy Spirit?

I tell you the truth
   ... and I believe You, Lord.
Anything you ask of the Father in My name, He will give to you!
   Ask and you will receive so that you will be filled with joy.
Asking is easy, Lord. Asking in Your name is another entire
   aspect of prayer. And this has produced faith, hope, and love
   ... and more often than not, persistent prayer.

I love persistent prayer.

- The time
- The trials
- The tests
- The triumphs!

For someone as engaged in prayer as I am,
  someone who loves to pray as much as I do,
    someone whose best moments are curled up in a prayer
    chair—
There are still times when I need my heart strengthened.

I love microwaving. I love high-speed internet. I love
instant answers to prayers. But that isn't always the case with
prayer, is it? Most of the time we need to persist in our prayer
assignments; we need to remain faithful to pray for the people
or specific things God has asked us to pray for. We need to
stand and when there is nothing left to do, remain standing
(Ephesians 6:13).

The strength to persist doesn't come without challenges,
frustrations, disappointments, or hopelessness. In reality,
healings don't come, marriages fall apart, prodigals don't come
home, and governments legislate ungodly principles. There is so
much heartache and pain.

However, over the years I have learned to find God in the
valley of unanswered prayers. I have learned to value the search
for the hidden treasures in delayed answers. Both have helped
me learn to hear the voice of God in the darkest of times.

> Let us not become weary in doing good, for at the proper
> time we will reap a harvest if we do not give up
> (Galatians 6:9 NIV).

There are times we go before the Lord and consider why our prayers are not being answered: "Am I praying wrong? Is my heart right? Is there something else I need to be praying?" We become weary in doing good.

When I come to that place, I inquire of the Lord. However, the question isn't "Why aren't my prayers being answered?" Rather, "How can I pray differently? Lord, what is it that You would like me to pray that will give life to this situation? Give hope to this person who has an illness? Give encouragement? Edify? What can I say, Lord, and what can I do to pray and be strengthened in my prayers?" I have discovered God is always ready to answer the prayer about how I can remain faithful and how I can be more persistent.

I've been known to be a bit of a pit bull when it comes to prayer requests. I love the challenges of prayer. I love knowing God's heart and God's will for a situation or circumstance. And even in the midst of unanswered prayer, I love the tenacity part. I love that God finds me trustworthy and faithful to dig in for those hidden treasures, to dive into His Word, and to pray in the Spirit to find the things He is saying about the person, city, situation, or thing going on in my life. Sometimes this doesn't resolve right away. Sometimes I trudge through seasons that require pressing through and wrestling to get to that place of peace with God, where we are synced together for the things I'm praying about.

My heart is etched with lists of people for whom I have prayed for over 20-plus years. There have certainly been times over those two decades when I have thought, "Wow, I'm just not getting through. I'm not breaking through." In those times of persistent prayer, I have asked the Lord to help me see things His way. When I start seeing things His way—versus filtering it through my own mind, soul, and spirit—I'm encouraged because God sees things with perfect love.

Whenever we are in a place of heaviness in our prayer life, we need to go to the Word of God to be encouraged. The Father is there with manna (the Word) for the morning, the evening, or whenever we need it to help us press through. There are several Scriptures that have helped me whenever I get to that place of wanting to break through in the area of persistent prayer. I want you to know that when you are involved in this area of pressing in, you are not alone. In prayer we engage the Father, the Son, and the Holy Spirit.

> My life dissolves *and* weeps itself away for heaviness; raise me up *and* strengthen me according to [the promises of] Your word (Psalm 119:28 AMPC).

The Father is always willing to strengthen us!

Then I love to turn to where Jesus says to Peter:

> "Simon, Simon (Peter) listen! Satan has asked excessively that [all of] you be given up to him [out of the power and keeping of God] that he might sift [all of] you like grain" (Luke 22:31 AMPC).

Have you ever felt like you're on the sifting board? It's not very fun, and it's kind of lonely. But Jesus follows this statement with, "But I have prayed especially for you [Peter]" (Luke 22:32 AMPC). That's where I like to insert my name:

> "I've prayed especially for you, *Mary Jo*. I have prayed that your own faith may not fail and when you have returned to Me, strengthen and establish your brethren."

I'm not alone! Jesus ever lives to intercede for me. That means I'm living from the finished work of the cross! I love that.

In Romans 8:26, the apostle Paul writes about the Holy Spirit—our Counselor, our Friend who sticks closer than a brother:

> In the same way, the Spirit helps us in our weakness. We do not know what we ought to pray for, but the Spirit himself intercedes for us through wordless groans (NIV).

You are not alone. When you carry the prayer assignments and burdens God has put on your heart—those righteous burdens—it's a joy to partner with the Lord on earth. When you are wrestling and trying to get to that place of peace—that place of comfort, that place of breakthrough, that place of really echoing the heart of God in the situation—get back to the Word. Ask the Lord to strengthen you as you read. Jesus has interceded with the finished work of the cross, and the Holy Spirit is there to help us in our weakness.

There are so many Scriptures on "strengthen." If "strengthen" is a vitamin you need to take for your prayer life, go to the Word. Search for "strengthen" in your concordance and be encouraged by the Lord!

> The eyes of the Lord search the whole earth in order to strengthen those whose hearts are fully committed to him (2 Chronicles 16:9 NLT).

> I can do all things through Christ who strengthens me (Philippians 4:13 NKJV).

Let me pray over you.

> I thank You, Lord, that there is nothing You have asked us to do and there is no place of faith You have asked us

to stand where fear is allowed to have a foothold. You are strengthening us in the Spirit. Just as You strengthened Elijah—just as You fed him when he endured and pressed in for 40 days, just as Your presence came to him—strengthen us that way, too. That faith will fill our prayers. We can do all things through Christ who strengthens us. Thank You, Lord. We depend and rely on You for this.

"Therefore strengthen the hands which hang down, and the feeble knees" (Hebrews 12:12 NKJV).

Lord, often our hands hang down because of the weariness and the weightiness of what we carry. But when we pray, our hands are lifted up to You. Lord, this, in itself, is a sign of surrender and acceptance, of receiving Your strength.

Father, I'm asking for Your perfect will to be done.
Jesus, I'm asking for Your Word not to return void but to do all that it is set out to accomplish.
Holy Spirit, I'm asking for Your power to perform the will and word of God.
Mary, I love it when you engage in Trinity-praying. This is a picture of unity, of being One with Me.

Even now, the Holy Spirit wants to encourage you in persisting in prayer. In staying the course, fighting the good fight, wrestling, and not letting go of God's promises and purposes. Even now, the Helper comes to bless you and speak life to your prayers. Even now.

JOHN 17

Our Mission

There are so many conversations—withdrawing to lonely places, early in the morning mountain prayer times—Jesus had with the Father and the Holy Spirit that are not recorded in Scripture. So many. More than not. I've always wanted to eavesdrop on talks among the Trinity during the 40 days Jesus spent in the wilderness. Or when Moses stood in front of the burning bush or lingered in the tent of meeting or fasted for 40 days…

Although we don't have the word-for-word conversations, we do know the fruit of these encounters. How strengthened, empowered, and purposed Jesus, Moses, Abraham, Elijah, Paul… (well, the list is long) were when leaving a presence-driven encounter with our Living God.

Now, in John 17, the Holy Spirit journals for you and me Jesus' prayer. We are left to hover over these words like the Spirit hovers over creation. Like He hovers over you and me as we read these words. Jesus definitely had you and me on His heart.

It is an incredible blessing to be on the giving and receiving ends of prayer. And here we are in one of the most beloved chapters in all of Scripture—John 17. Jesus is praying for you and me.

This prayer is also for all the believers who will follow them and hear them speak (John 17:20).

I love praying for other people. Connecting God to situations and circumstances. Engaging Him in what often seems impossible. And when I'm on the receiving end of prayer … well, it's so humbling, and I'm so grateful. I really need praying friends. It always settles my spirit, encourages my faith, and infuses me with strength.

Praying friends are a gift from God—people who will believe for you, stand in the gap for you, and cry out to God for you. People of faith. People who believe prayer makes a difference. People who believe in the power of agreement between God and man to bring God's will from heaven to earth.

It is said that more prayer is caught than taught. This is because teaching is often so cerebral. It's information, facts, truths, and data. It may include testimonies and statements of answered prayer as well as what you learn from unanswered prayers. But there is nothing like being around prayer that is Spirit-led, Word-based, and echoing the Father's heart and will. Whether it's on the phone, with a friend one-on-one, in a small group, around a gathering table, in churches, or even stadiums … When voices unite in agreeing prayer, there is nothing like it. It passes the head, enters the heart, and fills the spirit. You know it when you hear it.

Prayer!

Please read all of John 17. All 26 verses. Read it to yourself. Read it out loud. Read it slowly. Record it and listen to your recording. Plant these words deep in your spirit, your heart, and your mind. Let the Holy Spirit begin speaking to you.

Imagine sitting in your prayer chair and having Jesus sit there with you and pray for you.

Imagine John 17:

Jesus praying for His disciples.

That's you and me.

Jesus declares:

1. "You have entrusted Me with these men" (v. 6a).
2. "I have told them about Your nature and declared Your name to them" (v. 6b).
3. "They have held on to Your words and understood" (v. 6c).
4. "Not only understood them but also believed that You sent Me" (v. 8).

Jesus prays:

1. "As I return to be with You, holy Father, remain [abide] with them through Your name" (v. 11a).
2. "May they be one even as We are one" (v. 11b).
3. "I am speaking this prayer ... so that in hearing it they might be consumed with joy" (v. 13).
4. "Protect them from the evil one" (v. 15).
5. "Immerse them in the truth" (v. 17).
6. "I am sending them" (v. 18).
7. "I have set Myself apart so that they may be set apart by truth" (v. 19).
8. "This prayer is also for all the believers who will follow" (v. 20).
9. "By this unity the world will believe that You sent Me" (v. 21).
10. "All the glory You have given to Me, I pass on to them" (v. 22a).
11. "May that glory unify them" (v. 22b).
12. "You love them in the same way You love Me" (v. 23).

13. "I long for the time when those You have given Me can join Me" (v. 24).

Even as I make this list, the words penetrate my heart and fill me with joy, peace, and His love for you and me.

Linger, dear ones. Read and pray and breathe in Jesus' ultimate desire for you and me.

Dearest Lord Jesus,
I began this journey through John birthed out of the desire to
    know You more. To walk with You. To talk with You. And
    now to pray with You. These words in John 17 hover over
    me, and the Spirit rests on me, on these words, on these
    prayers, and on these requests You have made to the Father
    on my behalf. I'm overcome with the weightiness.
I feel like Moses … and Your glory has passed before me.
Hide me, Jesus, in the cleft of Your rock.
Dearest Mary,
It pleases Me to see answered prayer in you.
    To have you carry My heart for the Church, the lost, the
    hurting, the sick, the lonely …
Jesus,
I do feel a lot like Moses right now,
    Exodus 33 ringing in my ears, resounding in my spirit.
Tent of meeting,
    Face-to-face, just as a friend speaks to another friend.
You know my name, and You trust me. Reveal Your way to me.

    "My presence will go *with you*, and I will give you rest"
    (Exodus 33:14 NKJV).

Let me see Your glory
    Goodness and glory … passing before me right now.

Mary,

Come. Follow Me.

Lord,

Finishing well is so important to me. When my time has come, I want to look back and see a life that glorified You. I grew up saying this prayer:

> Glory be to the Father
> and to the Son and to the Holy Spirit.
> As it was in the beginning,
> is now,
> and ever shall be,
> world without end. Amen.[1]

And this is my prayer today.

I want my life to reflect Your goodness, Your attributes, Your character, Your love.

Mary, simply put, I came to glorify My Father and redeem mankind. That was My mission.

Jesus: I have glorified You on earth and fulfilled the mission You set before Me (John 17:4).

Everything I did and said supported bringing the Father glory and reuniting man to God.

And now the Father will glorify Me, and the Spirit will show you how to glorify Us (John 17:5).

I want the same thing for you, Mary. I want you to be one who stands before Me and says, "I have fulfilled the mission You set before me."

Oh Lord Jesus,

---

[1] *Gloria Patri*, Public Domain.

That is my heart's cry. I want Your mission to be my mission. Through these chapters in John, You have shown me *how.* You have shed light on my weaknesses and blessed my strengths. You have been my Savior, Shepherd, and Friend. Now, through prayer, I want to connect people to God the Father, Son, and Holy Spirit and glorify the Trinity.

Mary, follow Me.

Glory and Anointing

The Lord directed me to Isaiah 60 and 61.

- Isaiah 60 is about His glory.
- Isaiah 61 is about His anointing.

Mary,

First My glory, then My anointing. When you seek to glorify Me in all you do and say, the anointing will follow. Not anointing for anointing's sake; rather, anointing to …

> The Spirit of the Lord, the Eternal, is on me.
> *The Lord has appointed me for a special purpose.*
> He has anointed me to bring good news to the poor.
> He has sent me to repair broken hearts,
> And to declare to those who are held captive and bound in prison,
> "Be free *from your imprisonment!*" (Isaiah 61:1–3).

Lord, I feel like David:

> You have said, "Seek my face."
> My heart says to you,
> "Your face, Lord, do I seek" (Psalm 27:8 esv).

And that's why I'm here today. To seek Your face.
Mary, I

> "will be to you an everlasting light,
> And your God your glory" (Isaiah 60:19 NKJV).

When your time has come, these Scriptures will have been a footprint to finishing well. There is much to ponder and pray in these chapters today, tomorrow, always.

> "Arise [from spiritual depression to a new life], shine [be radiant with the glory *and* brilliance of the Lord]; for your light has come,
>   And the glory *and* brilliance of the Lord has risen upon you" (Isaiah 60:1 AMP).

Beloved followers of Christ: this is you. Your special purpose. Your mission to glorify the Father. How that looks in your life will be unique to you—your heart and how you reflect Jesus day in and day out. Look no further than the mirror. Do not look at another's calling or anointing and think you will do just that. The function may be the same, the passion the same, the direction the same ... but the expression will be uniquely yours.

I just received an email from a friend who is moving to the Middle East. This move is an accumulation of 10 years of dreaming, planning, working, submitting, praying, and seeking godly counsel. Many have questioned why. It's simple. She is being *sent*.

So much of these last five chapters (John 13–17), as Jesus ministered and spoke to the apostles, is about your and my mission. The question is not *if* we are being sent but rather **where**.

It's exciting.

It's challenging.

Stretching. Uncomfortable. Hard. Trying. Warfare.
    But the rewards are eternal.

"As the Father has sent me, I am sending you"
(John 20:21 NIV).

But wait—I'm getting ahead of myself again.

When you're ready, let's move on to John 18. But not until
you are ready. This chapter is so important. You need to be *sent*
to the next chapter.

JOHN 18

Not My Will

The Garden. *Gethsemane.*

I've been there. I've sat under century-old olive trees, praying. I've lain before the Lord prostrate—as Jesus once did—crying out to Father for His will to be done in my life.

There, in the midst of huge, lumbering trees, like soldiers standing guard, the winter ground was barren. However, spring was coming. In the dirt fields were sprinkles of red poppies, each reminiscent of the blood and tears shed by Jesus in that very place. The ground splattered with red poppies ... with drops of blood.

> And being in anguish, he prayed more earnestly, and his sweat was like drops of blood falling to the ground (Luke 22:44 NIV).

The apostle John doesn't record the travail of tears, the absent prayer partners, or the agony of our Lord.

I cannot go on. I return to the other Gospels and read and weep.

Each account so full and abundant in teaching me about prayer.

I'm a visual person, so when I saw the movie *The Passion of Christ*, it opened my eyes to the depth and breadth of Jesus' prayer life and relationship with the Father. It left me weak, but at the same time, it strengthened me. That intimate connection is what God is calling you and me to.

May His will be done in and through our relationship with Him and our prayers in agreement with His will.

Lord Jesus,
We started our journey in John with You asking,

> What is it that you want? (John 1:38)

and then issuing the invitation, "Come ... *Follow Me.*" Here in John 18, I hear You ask,

> Whom are you looking for? (v. 4).
> Whom are you searching for? (v. 7).

Lord Jesus,
In this journey I have found You anew. I have learned so much about Your relationship with the Father. You have invited me into those conversations. You have included me in meeting with Your apostles, building ministry, representing the Father, introducing me to the Spirit.
The list goes on and on. But I feel like You have taken my heart and made it a tablet. Where You have written:

> "Write the vision
> And make it plain
> And when Mary Jo reads it, she will run with it"
> (Habakkuk 2:2 MJP).

Dear Mary,
First and foremost, your love has brought you here. To this place, to this time. And your obedience will move you forward into even greater plans I have for you. Greater things you will do.
So much was transferred here in the Garden.

So much imparted to you through My prayers and through
My tears.
You are like a well-watered garden, and much fruit will come
forth.
It will be for My glory!
And it will bring you much **joy**.

> When a man really gives up trying to make something
> out of himself—a saint, or a converted sinner, or a
> churchman (a so-called clerical somebody), a righteous
> or unrighteous man … and throws himself into the arms
> of God … then he wakes with Christ in Gethsemane.
> That is faith, that is metanoia and it is thus that he
> becomes a man and Christian.
>
> —Dietrich Bonhoeffer[1]

When the soldiers questioned Jesus, He answered, "I
AM" (John 18:5 isv).

I AM.
Mary, this is the answer to every question moving forward.
Many will ask, "Who is He? What does He teach? How
do you know He is all He says He is?" All those questions
people who are crying out for faith and hope and love have.
I AM is the answer.
This is whom people are seeking and searching for …
"I AM THAT I AM" (Exodus 3:14 kjv).

Oh Lord,
I remember we spent time talking about I AM. Is this what part

---

[1] Dietrich Bonhoeffer, *The Cost of Discipleship* (New York: SCM Press Ltd,
1959), 24.

of the journey was about? Not just my knowing You better
but my being able to make You known.
I love that.
I love that.
I love that.
That is so Your heart—
For others.
I will follow You in this.

> I was regretting the past and fearing the future. Suddenly
> my Lord was speaking:
> "My name is I AM." He paused. I waited. He contin-
> ued, "When you live in the past, with its mistakes and
> regrets, it is hard. I am not there. My name is not I
> WAS. When you live in the future, with its problems
> and fears, it is hard. I am not there. My name is not I
> WILL BE. When you live in this moment, it is not hard.
> I am here. My name is I AM."
>
> —Helen Mallicoat[2]

Pick Your Battles

Do you remember when Jesus spoke to us about not picking
up offenses? Well, He also has something to say about not
picking your battles.

In John 18:10, Peter comes to Jesus' defense. He picks up a
sword, and ready to do battle, he severs the right ear of a servant
of the high priest. But Jesus tells him to put the sword down.

---

[2] Helen Mallicoat, "I AM," in *Prayers for the Classroom*, ed. Philip Verhalen
(Collegeville: The Liturgical Press, 1998), 184.

Mary,

Pick your battles.

Lord, I hear you.

Mary,

First, know you are never alone.

The battle is Mine (2 Chronicles 20:15).

Then, Mary, do not be presumptuous.

Don't presume and throw Scriptures around like simple
bandages.

Seek Me.

Seek My will.

Seek My strategy.

Seek My Word.

Pick your battles and pick your weapons.

For the weapons of our warfare are not carnal, but
mighty through God to the pulling down of strong holds
(2 Corinthians 10:4 KJV).

Listen first.

I know the battles you will be facing,

you will be up against,

you will be confronted with.

I will often speak and sharpen your weapon even before you
know you have need of it.

Other battles, Mary,

are long and require endurance and faith and hope and love.

For those, Mary,

Always praise. Worship.

Maintain a fasting lifestyle.

Stay in the Word. Keep your heart from offenses.

Keep short accounts with Me.

Lord,

Here in the Garden, You were asked, "What do you teach?"
(John 18:19).

Lord, these soldiers represent so many today. In the Garden,
filled with questions, accusations, hatred, unbelief. So many
in the valley of decision.

You have come to seek and save the lost.

I want my prayers and life to do the same.

Lord, going forth, in Your name,

with the Spirit to lead and guide and counsel and give
utterance …

"If anyone would come after me, let him deny himself
and take up his cross daily and follow me"
(Luke 9:23 ESV).

Always, Lord, looking, seeking, pursuing You!

I want to see You in every situation and circumstance,
every person, every relationship, every church service,
every prayer meeting, every … everything. Everywhere. All
the time.

Dear ones, there is something sacred about "yet not my will,
but yours be done" (Luke 22:42 NIV). And this is the heart
of John 18 for you: the place of ultimate surrender, drawing a
line in the sand, living outside your comfort zone, and literally
letting Jesus' light and glory shine through you.

As I finish writing this chapter, I have just returned from a
prayer pilgrimage to Israel. My tenth trip. Each one changed me,
but this one marked me—so much so that I have begun a fast. I
cannot move forward without more clarity, more purpose, and
more direction.

Lord Jesus,

As I lingered on my face before You

At En Gedi

Mt Carmel

Garden Tomb

Southern Steps

Mt Beatitudes

These and so many other *build an altar in my heart* places.

I want

I need

I desire

to move my spiritual address to a deeper place in
Your heart.

Help me, Holy Spirit, begin and finish this well.

Dear One,

I am the Anointed One,

and in this season of fasting, your heart's desire will be
realized.

You say *abide*, and I say *desire*.

Lord,

That blesses me. I want to fast to draw closer to You. Abide
in you. And yet You continue to bring my worship to a place
where You want to speak to me. It's about You!

Dear Mary,

It is about Me. Actually, it's about what I am doing in you.

If you let Me take the lead on this, your desire will be
transforming.

I'm about to surprise you.

Thank You, Lord!

My desire for you and your desire for Me.

We've talked about it, Mary, and now we are going to live it in new ways.

You will love the fruit.

I'm ready. Willing and able.

So am I!

Your Garden encounter, dear ones, begins with "not my will" and ends with a heart in sync with His.

Enjoy the surrender.

Be blessed in the commitment.

Live out His desire for you.

JOHN 19

What's in Your Hand

In John 19, Jesus is characteristically silent. He does not defend Himself. He doesn't argue or take the bait. Instead, He simply states the profound truth that the ultimate authority any of us have comes from the Father.

The one who handed Me to you is guilty of the greater sin
    (John 19:11).

What caught my eye was the word *handed.* It took me back to the first page of my journal when the Holy Spirit highlighted *hands.*

Mary, what is in your hand?
    Right now, Lord … it's Your Word.
Do you know what I see? I see clean hands and a pure heart.
    I see My Word … your hugging Bible, filling your hands.
    I see 5 fingers twice. Five representing grace.
And I say double grace to you …
    Grace to the mountains before you.
    Grace to speak to that mountain.
    Grace to not go around that mountain again.
Grace freely receive … in your hands and by your hands freely give.
    Part of this fast, Mary, is how I want to use your hands:
        To lay hands on the sick,
            To pray,

To write,
  To bake,
    To make.
I told you there would be some surprises, and there will be.
  Now hold on to that hugging Bible as I reset the rhythm of
  your life.
Lord,
Proverbs 31 speaks of eager hands, willing hands: "Works with
  her hands in delight" (v. 13 NASB). I've given You my heart
  and now my hands.

What's in your hands? Proverbially. Literally. Spiritually. God is ready to take what you have in your hands and, like the fish and loaves, pray over them, bless them, and give to the hungry, needy world. What's in your hands?

Jesus was handed over to be crucified.

What looked like the ultimate failure was the crowning triumph of His life.

What looked like loss was gain.

What looked like darkness and defeat was light and victory!

There on the cross was the greatest act of intercession: mediating on our behalf.

In his book *Intercessory Prayer,* Dutch Sheets describes what happened as our Jesus hung on the cross, prepared to give up His life for you and me.

- Mercy *met* judgment.
- Righteousness *met* sin.
- Light *met* darkness.
- Humility *met* pride.

- Love *met* hate.
- Life *met* death.
- A cursed One on a tree *met* the curse that originated from a tree.[1]

There on the cross—no better example of Jesus fully human and fully divine.

John records two statements from Jesus as He hung on the cross that spoke to me of His humanity:

1. The care of "Dear woman" (v. 26).
2. The declaration (not request) "I am thirsty" (v. 28).

There on the cross we witness the *greater love.*

> "Greater love has no one than this: to lay down one's life for one's friends" (John 15:13 NIV).

Jesus (*to Mary, His Mother*): Dear woman, this is your son ... (to *John*, His disciple) This is now your mother (John 19:26–27).

Lord Jesus,
This touches me deeply.
I didn't have family in the birthing kind of way. Never pregnant. Never bone of my bone. Never flesh of my flesh.
And yet You saw fit to pick up the broken pieces of my life and give me family.
I have the family. You gave them to me. And through these beloved members—husband, children, grandchildren—I have learned love.
So Jesus, on the cross when You look down at beloved ones

[1] Dutch Sheets, *Intercessory Prayer: How God Can Use Your Prayers to Move Heaven and Earth* (Grand Rapids, MI: Bethany House Publishers, 1996), 51.

and pronounce *family*, it deeply moves me. Covenant
relationships.

Mary,

This was a very personal

and intentional

act of love as I hung on the cross.

I spoke and affirmed relationships.

Mary would be rightly connected all the days of her life.

And so will you.

So be it.

Families

Lord, relationships get complicated.

I want to guard my heart and mind from others' anger but at
the same time hear their pain and own my failures. I trust, by
the Spirit, I will

Not hide

but remain hidden in You.

Not denial

but discernment.

Not retreat

but renew.

I know You can make all things new again. And my prayer is for
God-ordained, God-fulfilled, God-blessed relationships.

Will we ever fully grasp, understand, or have complete revelation of the cross? I think not. There are so many awestruck
wonders about Jesus' life.

- God who became man
- Born of a virgin
- Completely human

- Completely God
- Perfect
- Without sin
- Continual communion with the Father and the Holy Spirit
- Baptism
- Suffering
- Cross
- Resurrection
- Supernatural
- Scriptures fulfilled

Jesus,
I have no words. I'm not a bystander watching a crucifixion. I'm
not a casual observer to a brutal, merciless torture of a man.
I'm not a spectator who has no interest in who, what, why.
You are my Lord. You are my Redeemer. You are my Savior.
And You called me *Friend.*
Mary, Dear One,
I would do it again if need be.
But there is no need be.
When I declared, "It is finished," that is what it means for
eternity.
My work is finished.
Yours has begun, and together we move forward.

As I walked through these last days with Jesus, I was
profoundly impacted by the truth of "I will never leave you nor
forsake you" (Hebrews 13:5 NKJV). My response to the Lord is,
"I will never leave You nor forsake You."

What about you? Are there times when you have felt alone
or abandoned? That you went to your cross alone? Let the

Spirit of God minister to you and bring healing, hope, and health.

Thirsty

Lord Jesus,
I don't understand, even in a small way, what that must have
  been like to be so thirsty.
    Is it that when we are carrying our cross we feel thirsty? Dry?
    Parched?
There on the cross, physically beaten and bruised
    for my transgressions—sins—
      Such thirst.
    And still refuse any liquid that would dull Your pain, relieve
    the thirst?
    Is it because when I am dry and thirsty
      no liquid could refresh, replenish, or restore me ...
        Only the living water that comes from You.
Quenching my thirst comes from doing the will of the Father,
    following Jesus with the Helper!
Indeed. You get it. You get Me. You get Us!
This takes us back to John 4:12. The well. I am the living water.
    You are right to revisit how to move forward.
    I will always be the answer to our dry dessert, wilderness,
    pain, heartache, doubt, and confusion....
    It will always be Me!
Moving forward we will be more intentional.
    You are going to practice what you preach!
    You are going to be your best student.

Yes, Lord. You just made me laugh! I have the best teacher. You. I want to be one of Your star pupils.

Earlier this year I declared over you *enough is enough!* The war is over.

You have re-enlisted, renewed, and now with this last 40-day fast. Realigned.

The war is over.

Now as we approach the end of this year … you will declare, IT IS FINISHED!

There is a peace, Jesus, that what You say is true. We are about to close this chapter and begin a new season. Have I told You how blessed I am that this journey through John was not as I planned but became what You desired? Not 21 days. No way. This lingering journey has truly transformed me. Have I told you today *thank You?*

Cody Carnes wrote a beautiful song filled with truth and hope and love: "The Cross Has The Final Word."[2] *Final*: unchangeable, nonnegotiable, crowning. My Prince of Peace endured a crown of thorns so that I could have a crown of life. Oh, what a beautiful glimpse of His love!

From the darkness of the crucifixion to the light of the resurrection …

When you are ready, let's move on to John 20—another garden! Not Gethsemane; rather, the garden tomb. But still, "His will be done."

---

[2] Cody Carnes, "The Cross Has The Final Word," in *The Darker The Night/ The Brighter The Morning*, Carnes Music Group LLC, 2017, CD.

JOHN 20

Before the sun had risen on Sunday morning …
John 20:1

My heart leaps.

Awake. Arise. Abide.

For 10-plus years I was responsible for overseeing the prayer and intercession department of my church. At the end of every year, I would gather my leadership team, and we would seek God about a focus for the upcoming year. One year the prophetic words were *Awake Arise Abide.*

I was reminded of those words as I looked at John 20 and revisited the appointment at the garden tomb. *Awake Arise Abide* was the three-cord strand Jesus was weaving into me on this journey through the Gospel of John.

Lord Jesus,
   I love this conversation
      at the tomb.
   While all the others were hiding,
      fearful of the pending doom,
   You lingered to speak
      to one sobbing and sad,
   Words of hope and life
      that made her heart glad.

199

Mary,
You've stayed behind
  so many times.
  You've lingered for
  a touch, a word, a whisper.
  You've lingered
      in our prayer room,
      in our church,
      in conversations,
      in teaching,
      in mentoring.
        You stop and linger.
  You wait to hear My voice.
    You allow Me to interrupt where you are going, what you
    are doing, when you're speaking …
  You've lingered.
  The Spirit has hovered.
  And in that lingering you have learned to hear Me call your
  name.
Lord,
This conversation always leaves me breathless.
  Mary sobbing … distraught … troubled.
  So much so she did not recognize You.
  Oh, I know those feelings.
  Oh, I know how that could happen.
  Oh, I know the suddenness of Your presence that casts out
  all doubts and fears and tears …
  When I hear You call my name.
  Mary.
Mary.
Yes, my Lord.

Awake Arise Abide.
Now go tell your brothers and sisters.
   Tell all I send you to.
   Tell what you have learned.
   Give away what you have been given.
   Multiplied like the fish and loaves.
You will always, always, always have enough to give.
   Awake
   Arise
   Abide
And Mary … be at peace.
I am sending you now.
   Your life of prayer, your living prayer, your prayers will make
   a way.
I will, Lord. I will.

     I will be fully satisfied when I awake in the morning,
     seeing You face-to-face and
     having sweet communion with You
     (Psalm 17:15 MJP—my life Scripture).

Linger saints. Outside the garden tomb. Often times we are looking for God in our lives, and He is right there in plain sight, yet we don't see Him. Today Jesus is calling your name. Today He is affirming your call. Today He is saying to each of you:
Awake.
Arise.
Abide.
A peaceful settling in my spirit today.
   Not because of any particular
      person,

project,
or plan.
But rather a peaceful presence ... lingering, hovering, covering of my
God:
Father,
Son,
Holy Spirit.
I was led to look up Isaiah 4:5–6.

Mary,
I am creating you to be a dwelling place of My presence:
As the cloud by day and the fire by night,
You will carry My presence.
You will be for others ...
a place of refuge,
a shelter from the storm.
"And I will be a wall of fire all around you, and I will be the glory
in your midst" (Zechariah 2:5 paraphrase).
Beloved, there will be many doubters, skeptics, non-believers.
All I'm asking of you ...
is to be you and let Me be Me in you.
Thy word and Thy will be done.
That's what I thought you would say.
I love you.
I love you, Lord.

Can you imagine anything more miraculous?
A crucified Savior.
A resurrected King.
And here at the most heart-wrenching turned

heart-awakening time, Jesus meets with His disciples. They were locked away in fear. Sound familiar?

Fear locking us up.

Fear blocking our anointing.

Fear weighing us down.

Fear keeping us from our destiny.

Let it not be. Do not move past this upper room encounter where Jesus is sending His disciples with a mantle to co-represent Him.

Jesus: I give you the gift of peace. In the same way the Father sent Me, I am now sending you (John 20:21).

But wait! Verse 22 says, "He drew close enough to each of them that *they could feel His breath*". This sending comes with the breath of God, the Holy Spirit. Think on this.

༄

Any doubts like Thomas? Deal with them now. Address even the deepest doubts or fears. God wants to meet with you and breathe Holy Spirit life into your heart and awaken your spirit!

JOHN 21

Breaking Day

What a journey we have been on together. Each of us on our own personal walks with Jesus through the Gospel of John. And now we find ourselves in Tiberias, a town on the western shore of the Sea of Galilee.

Not long ago, I was sitting on a wall overlooking these waters and imagining the event that John records in chapter 21. To my left was a larger-than-life statue of Jesus telling Peter to "Feed My sheep." To my right was the shoreline filled with families and tourists enjoying the peaceful end of a long day. The sun was setting, and the light reflecting off the sea was a glistening, life-filled picture of Jesus walking on these waters.

As I read John 21, I wondered anew how the disciples who walked with Jesus for three years did not recognize Him. Much like Mary as she approached the "gardener." Many theologians have written opinions on these verses. But for you and me, it is better to sit and ponder this journey and reflect how by the Spirit of God, we have grown to know His voice and recognize His presence.

Lord Jesus,
    When was it? What chapter? Verse? Moment?
        When I,
            lingering longer,
            listened closer,
            leaned into my Beloved.

I can't pinpoint an exact time when
Your *presence* transformed,
transitioned,
translated this one from
one who seeks, knock, asks
to one who walks hand in hand,
abiding face-to-face,
moving forward shoulder-to-shoulder.
Your *presence* made all the difference.

Daughter Dear,
There was a time,
a moment,
a season,
a reason I said NOW!
Now birth her,
breathe life into her,
release her to see.
The years have passed quickly.

There was a time,
a moment,
a season,
a reason I said NOW!
Now birth her,
breathe anointing into her,
release her to be.

There is a time,
a moment,
a season,
a reason I say NOW!

Now birth her,
   breathe destiny into her,
      release her to Me.

The days ahead are planned by Me,
An unfolding of your destiny.
You have been tried and tested,
And now you are fully vested.

Follow Me all the days ahead.
   Many will follow in your stead.
My presence will go with each one
   As My work on earth is done.

You and I have come so far in our walks through the
Gospel of John. Can we possibly go back to where we were
at the start? Not after encountering the presence of God in
the Scriptures. Not after the conversations, the lingering, the
listening.

Scripture tells us,

> They went out in the boat and caught nothing through the
> night. As day was breaking ... (John 21:3b–4).

Saints, can I say *our day* is breaking?

In this journey Jesus has taught us how to hear His voice and
follow Him. The Spirit of God quickens us to hear and obey.
Of all the accounts of Peter, this is one of my favorites:

The disciple loved by Jesus turned to Peter and said:

Beloved Disciple: It is the Lord.

Immediately, when Simon Peter heard these words, he threw on his shirt (which he would take off while he was working) and dove into the sea (John 21:7).

- "dove into the sea" (MSG)
- "jumped into the water" (NLT)
- "threw himself into the sea" (ESV)
- "sprang into the sea" (AMPC)
- "cast himself into the sea" (KJV)
- "plunged into the sea" (CSB)

However the translation states it, there is no question Peter would have walked on water to get to Jesus this time. What faith. What a beautiful spontaneous response. What JOY!

And because we know what's coming … what redemption.

Dear Lord Jesus,

My heart is so full as we come to the end of this particular journey through John. I want to be like Peter at the Mount of Transfiguration and say, "Can't we just camp here forever? Eat the fish of Your provision and the bread of Your presence?"

I can't imagine going back. That's not Your plan. And it's not my plan.

Mary,

Yes. You can camp here.

You can continually be fed by My provision and the bread of My presence.

In fact, it's the thread of these chapters that have brought you to this place.

You will hear My voice saying, "Throw your net here …" and whether that is calling you to your tent of meeting, to prayer, to teaching, to baking bread, to _____, it is My voice calling you to follow Me.

The Last Meal

There on the shores of the Sea of Tiberius, Jesus once again took fish and loaves and gave them to His disciples. How fitting—how Jesus—that this last meal was another fish and loaves story. This time, though, the fish is what we have in our hands, provided by the direction of our Lord, and the bread is provided by the Lord. The fish and the bread of His presence.

And there on that same shore, sitting on the wall, I took communion.

Bread.

Bread of His Presence.

And I reflected on the meal Jesus prepared for His disciples in this place.

Jesus,

This meal. This fish and loaves. You have taken what I have caught at Your direction. This reminds me of the fish and loaves that You multiplied and fed the multitudes. I am reminded, Lord: You do so much with my so little.

Mary,

Take communion with Me often.

Pause for Shabbat and keep the Sabbath holy.

Break bread with your fellow sojourners.

Share in the fruit of your labors.

Live from the pace and rhythm I've shown you.

Live well.

Love well.

I will, Lord. As for me and my house, my heart, my prayer life,
I will serve the Lord.

_____, do you love Me?

_____, do you love Me?

_____, do you love Me?

Lord, as for me and my house, my heart, in and through my
prayer life, I will serve You.

I know when I ask you if you love Me, I will hear, "You know I
love You." And I do.

So _____,

Take care of My lambs.

Shepherd My sheep.

Look after My sheep.

I will, Lord.

Follow Me.

> Give me your lantern and compass,
> give me a map,
> So I can find my way to the sacred mountain,
> to the place of your presence,
> To enter the place of worship,
> meet my exuberant God (Psalm 43:3–4 MSG).

And You did, Lord.

I love You, Lord.

I love you, Mary

It's time to say *Amen.* For now. For this journey. If I could type slower and make this moment with you last, I would. May you continue searching the Scriptures, finding your name, your compass, your light. May you continually be filled with the presence of God. May your tomorrows be enriched through all we have journeyed and may many follow you as you follow Him. Amen, dear ones. Amen.

> That his prayer was nothing else but a sense of the presence of GOD, his soul being at that time insensible to everything but Divine love: and that when the appointed times of prayer were past, he found no difference, because he still continued with GOD, praising and blessing Him with all his might, so that he passed his life in continual joy.[1]

---

[1] Brother Lawrence, *The Practice of the Presence of God: The Best Rule of Holy Life* (Xulon Press, 2017), 22.

EPILOGUE

We were standing on a high place overlooking the ground that had been the battlefield during the Six-Day War of 1967. Israeli soldiers had fought and died to capture and secure this network of Syrian fortifications. Brave soldiers gave their lives to secure the promises of God. Here at Tel Faher, a memorial site had been erected to remember and honor the lives lost.

We took a moment of silence to remember the fallen soldiers and prayed for their families and those serving in the IDF.

Ilan Barkay, our tour guide, spoke with great solemnity and passion. He gave us insight into the character, core, and courage of the Israeli military. He spoke about the generals and said, "Our leaders, our generals, do not send their soldiers into battle. They go before them. They do not prepare strategy and then have others carry it out. They do not go without having assessed the cost—they lead the way. They go first. They are in front. The soldiers follow."

It reminded me of our Jesus. In the Gospel of John, after His first words ("What do you seek?"), is "Follow Me." Then the last words He speaks in John 21 are "Follow Me." Jesus never intended for us to go into battle alone. He came to show us the way and go before us. He came with the strategy of heaven: *Your will, not mine; if this cross could pass; I only do what the Father tells me to do; love first; forgive much; healing* … and on and on.

Jesus showed us how to go to the cross—He went to the cross.

Jesus showed us how to die—He died on the cross.

Jesus showed us how to live—He rose to live as we will live.

My husband, an American history professor, said, "The greatest military leaders were those who would not ask their men to do anything they wouldn't do. Patton … They're in the battle right alongside their men. George Washington …"

Our General, Our Savior, Our Redeemer went to the cross and invited us to follow Him. The cross was not the end; rather, the moment He said, "It is finished" was the beginning. Our failures and our dead-end attempts—when we lived in darkness and brokenness—are the past, and **it is finished**. Jesus invites us to follow Him.

Yes, the battles are there. But we are assured He goes before us. We are assured the Holy Spirit counsels and directs, encourages and strengthens us. We are assured of His will being done through us.

We simply respond to *Come. Follow Me.*

NOTE FROM THE AUTHOR

My first book is titled *Adventures in Prayer: A 40-Day Journey*.

When I began writing *Follow Me as I Follow Jesus*, the Lord reminded me that this was actually going to be my first book. However, I was clearly redirected by the Lord. He said, "First things first."

Today, as I finished the last chapter of this book, I found this journal entry:

Lord, You said *Adventures in Prayer* was Your gift to me, and this book will be my gift to You.

Mary, this gift you are preparing for Me:

"My joy will be made full and complete and perfect in this journey through John. The readers will experience My delight fulfilled in them. My enjoyment will be perfected in their body, soul, and spirit. And they will have My gladness with them, filling their hearts" (John 17:13 MJP).

So be it Lord,
Amen.

APPENDIX

Mary Jo's Honey Challah

INGREDIENTS

- 5 tsp. (or two packages) active dry yeast
- 1 cup warm water (115°F)
- 1/4 cup honey (1 Tbsp. reserved for yeast)
- 1/4 cup sugar
- 5 cups bread flour
- 2 tsp. salt
- 3 eggs slightly beaten, plus 1 egg intended for glaze
- 8 Tbsp. (1 stick) unsalted butter, melted and cooled*
- Honey crystals, poppy seeds, or sesame seeds (optional)
- Prayers

DIRECTIONS:

Step 1: In warm water add the yeast and 1 Tbsp. honey. Stir. Let stand **until foamy**, about 5–10 minutes. Tip: Heat and sweet activate the yeast. If no foam, start again, as yeast could be old, and your bread will not rise.

Step 2: Using a stand mixer with a dough hook on low speed, mix 4 cups of bread flour, 2 tsp. salt, and ¼ cup sugar. Add the wet ingredients (yeast, egg, butter, and remaining honey) to the dry ingredients. Then add the additional 1 cup of bread flour as needed until the dough separates from the side of bowl and climbs the dough hook.[†]

Step 3: Knead the dough (approximately 100 times or 5–10 minutes) until it is not sticky and forms a silky like ball (add dusted flour as necessary). **Use this time to pray. For the people who will partake of this bread. For Israel and the families as they make their challah and prepare for Shabbat. For whomever and whatever God puts on your heart.** Press the dough down with your finger to see if it bounces back. Form the dough into a ball and lightly gloss the dough with oil. Transfer it to a lightly oiled bowl.[‡] Cover the bowl with a kitchen towel and let it rise in a warm area for 1:45–2 hours.

Step 4: Punch down the dough (this removes air bubbles) and place on counter. Use cutter to divide the dough equally into six sections.[§] Roll each section into a cord about 12–15 inches long. Braid *two* 3-cord loaves.[ℂ] Place the loaves on an oiled baking sheet, and cover with a kitchen towel. Let the dough rise until the loaves double in size, about 60 minutes.

Step 5: Preheat oven to 350°F. Gently brush the bread with a beaten egg and sprinkle honey crystals, poppy seeds, or sesame seeds (optional toppings). Place bread loaves on lower third of oven for 25 to 35 minutes. Internal temperature should be 200 degrees. **Tip:** If the bread is browning too quickly, tent with aluminum foil.

Let them cool completely on a wire rack (if you can keep from tasting them right away!). *This recipe is made with love and served with joy.*

Yield: 2 Loaves

*My personal preference is to melt and cool the butter.

†If you don't have a mixer, add the dry and wet ingredients and then knead until the dough is silky smooth. It will take you longer, but it is very doable.

‡Oil the bowl and dough as this will prevent the dough from sticking to the side of the bowl and not rising.

§I use a scale to weigh the cords. This makes for a more uniform braid, but it is not essential.

ⱯBraid as you would a hair braid. YouTube has excellent demonstrations for all sorts of braids. Have fun!

If you need assistance, my YouTube channel will walk you through this recipe. Just search www.YouTube.com/mjpraying.

TESTIMONIES

A man's steps *are* of the Lord;
How then can a man understand his own way?
   (Proverbs 20:24 NKJV).

The answer is through conversation with God!

As a spiritual mother to me, Mary Jo has helped me hear what the Spirit is saying and paved the way for my personal prayer life. I, in turn, teach this to my children and others. It is a legacy of living prayer.

Follow Me as I Follow Jesus is so timely. The moment I read the introduction—the invitation to talk with God—my heart leapt, and my spirit became hungry. Mary Jo invites us into some deep and intimate conversations, which inspire us to go to that secret place, Bible and pen in hand. We speak and then listen.

May our conversations with God be never-ending. May our spirits awake, arise, and abide in Him. And may we answer the invitation to "Follow Me," enduring to the end!

ROBERT SOCHA
Graduate | Christ for the Nations Institute
Husband | Father | Intercessor

Mary Jo Pierce is a pioneer of modern-day prayer. She has shown me how to ignite God's active responses to real life questions that bring peace and restoration to the broken pieces of our hearts.

Whether in her prayer room, on a rooftop gazing at the stars, or in Israel following the footsteps of Christ, Mary Jo has shown me what it means to walk with God and enjoy life even in the midst of pain.

I am endlessly grateful for her mentorship and her friendship. May the words of *Follow Me as I Follow Jesus* change your life as Mary Jo has changed mine. Pray on!

AUDREY COOK
Student | University of Texas at Dallas
Global Prayer Ambassador
International Blogger

Three years ago, Mary Jo invited me to begin meeting with her in her prayer room. I was a senior in high school, and I had no idea what God had in store for me!

Through Mary Jo's mentoring (and her overabundant supply of calligraphy pens), I began a journey of learning how to hear God through calligraphy and journaling. Having a conversation with God and His Word is prayer. Time and time again, I have watched Mary Jo go to the Word, exchange her questions for truth, and express it all through calligraphy. She taught me the beauty in praying and having one-on-one conversations with God through writing out my prayers and God's answers to them in my own calligraphy journal.

I remember a time when Mary Jo told me to make prayer the incense of my year. I did, and I now believe that prayer will be the incense of my life, thanks to the impact she has had on me. I pray your personal journey through *Follow Me as I Follow Jesus* will have the same life-changing impact.

MONIKA WIESINGER
Professional Photographer
Student | Texas A&M University
Lover of Jesus

Like many believers, I spent the first 30 years of my Christian walk letting the "experts" do the praying. They were the ones who could really reach God. I was not. Then I met Mary Jo Pierce. My life and my family's lives were changed forever.

When I first desired to obey Jesus' "Follow Me" 15 years ago, I realized it meant I needed to listen to what he Had to say. Mary Jo showed me, taught me, mentored me, pressed me, and encouraged me to talk to God, just as He talks to us in His Word. I have now spent 15 years growing closer to my Lord and leading my family and others to do the same. Praying now is truly without ceasing for me and those I can influence.

In the pages of *Follow Me as I Follow Jesus*, Mary Jo makes it possible for everyone to experience all those things that I did one-on-one with her as my prayer leader, teacher, mentor, and friend.

Thank you forever, Mary Jo!!

HOWARD WEISBERG
Intercessor | Israel and the Nations
Chairman and CEO | MC Materials

During a college summer break, I had one of those "happenings" Scripture tells us about—those unplanned yet God-planned, divine appointments. I interned with Mary Jo, and what I thought was only a summer interlude, I soon learned was also God's plan to build a foundation of living prayer and intercession in my life. I had the opportunity to deepen my relationship with the Lord by following her walk with Him.

Mary Jo has been the greatest influence in my prayer and worship life. She has taught me how to wait on the Lord through the importance of resting (a wonderful expression of prayer) and setting it as my foundation in ministry—and life!

I find her teaching me over and over again through *Follow Me*. She allows the Lord to use her breakthroughs to guide us readers in our walk of faith and encourages us to hold onto the dreams and promises God has put in our hearts. She teaches us to wait on the Lord for His perfect timing.

This book is your *happening*—your unplanned yet God-planned, divine appointment with God and the Scriptures. Pray on!

MADDISON HARRIS
Worship Leader | Prayer and Intercession
Intern for Life

Get excited about *Follow Me as I Follow Jesus*! I have known Mary Jo Pierce for 11 years, and I can unequivocally say she lives a lifestyle of prayer that is relevant, engaged, authentic, and pure. In the time I have known her, she has helped me live a lifestyle of prayer that is rich with integrity and authenticity, and more than once, she has revitalized my approach to God's Word. No matter where you are in your prayer life, this book will inspire, excite, and equip you with practical tools to grow in your intimacy with Jesus.

JAY BOGENREIF
Son | Husband | Father | Airline Pilot

I have "done life" with Mary Jo Pierce for over a decade now, and I am blessed to call her a friend, mentor, and pastor.

As my mentor, the very first assignment she ever gave me was to read the Gospel of John and write and personalize every Scripture as if God was speaking directly to me. The second assignment was to watch the movie *The Gospel of John*. These assignments took time, and I did them both more than once. Eventually I applied this principle to other books of the Bible as well.

Follow Me as I Follow Jesus will do this for you! Mary Jo does more than take you through her journals; she facilitates *your* stepping into Scripture. If you want to walk where Jesus walked, see through His eyes, and taste, touch, and *hear Him* in new ways, then this is how you start the journey.

CHRISTY ATKINSON
Intercessor | Revivalist

Over the years, I have ministered closely with Mary Jo, serving on her leadership team and being a Prayer Shield partner. Even after all this time, I still remember her very first prayer class in 2006. Why? Because there was an impartation for a desire to be still and hear God. That class set me on a quest to know God and put me on a path of prayer and intercession for others that will take me to eternity.

Follow Me as I Follow Jesus will do the same for you. There is an impartation awaiting each reader. This book is one of the clearest ways to really follow God's Word and know Him personally. I wish I could have read this when I was a teenager. It would have changed how I saw Jesus, the Father, and the Holy Spirit. I would have understood the gospel so much better. This is the best way I can imagine knowing God better and letting Him lead you where He wants you to go.

BOYD BASSHAM
Intercessor | John 17

Mary Jo Pierce is a rarity. I can honestly say she has influenced my prayer life more than any other person, simply by being "Mary Jo." She draws me in with the depth and tangibility of her prayer life and her joyful, adventurous journey with Jesus. She serves as a living expression of prayer and inspires me to live the same way.

Acting as a courier entrusted with hand-crafted divine invitations, Mary Jo has somehow done in *Follow Me as I Follow Jesus* what she does so well in person—leading us to Jesus and inviting us to step into His eternal storyline. In subtle yet profound ways, she baits us with questions, much like Jesus did. Before you know it, you are hooked, reeled, swept up into the boat, and at the mercy of the Fisherman.

It's amazing to me how little of "Mary Jo" I encounter in this book. Her deep passion to exhort and inspire others in living prayer demands her absence and makes way for God's heart, God's voice, and God's plans to transcend her every word—and penetrate our hearts directly. Clothed in infectious simplicity, Mary Jo inspires by way of demonstration.

"Living prayer" is simply being who we are, fully surrendered to Him.

PIA JO REYNOLDS
National Mobilization | Awaken the Dawn
Worship Leader | Intercessor

I've observed my Aunt Mary Jo's relationship with the Lord for at least two decades. As the Holy Spirit was depositing impressions on my heart and sealing them for future recollections, my faith was growing. On a trip to Dallas, Texas, in 2006, Mary Jo briefly showed me a prophetic poem and picture the Holy Spirit had given to her. I was amazed, intrigued, and curious. God was giving me a glimpse.

In 2013, when I heard the Holy Spirit's voice for the first time, my Aunt Mary Jo was the first person I called! In that moment, the Lord knit our spiritual hearts together. He began to write our kindred journey of prayer. Aunt Mary Jo has encouraged me to press in to God, to be still, and to listen. Like a spiritual heritage through the generations, the Lord has passed down a deep passion for prayer, a joy of living outside my comfort zone, and a great zeal for equipping others.

Follow Me as I Follow Jesus immediately drew me back to that powerful, intimate place with the Lord. Prayer, the Word, and journaling have always been essentials of mine, but this book rekindled a passion and reignited my prayer life in ways I didn't expect and couldn't imagine! It has fine-tuned my ears to hear His still, small voice. I know it will do the same for you!

KRISTA DOYLE
Homeschooling Mother | Professional Photographer
Prayer Partner

ACKNOWLEDGMENTS

The Lord bless you and keep you;
The Lord make His face shine upon you,
And be gracious to you;
The Lord lift up His countenance on you,
And give you peace.

Numbers 6:24–26 (NKJV)

There is a television commercial that begins by showing one person using a product and then reveals the vast number of people working behind the scenes to bring that product to completion. I hardly think of this book as a "product"—rather, it is an offering to the Lord—but it still took a team of gifted, praying, and believing-in-me people to produce what you are now holding. To each I owe a deep debt of gratitude.

To those who worked tirelessly to see this stepping-into-Scripture journey transferred from the pages of my journal to the pages of this book:

- Thank you to John Andersen, who can hear an idea and then with lightning speed put the vision into action. He has taught me so much about loving and caring (and praying) for my readers.
- Thank you to Jenny Morgan, my editor. In the natural I watched this young mother walk through her first

pregnancy and bring precious Lucy into this world. Such love, care, and joy went into every aspect of her daughter's growth, and we rejoiced together at seeing the fulfillment of what God created in her. I observed the same love, care, and joy as Jenny worked on this manuscript. With integrity for the heart of the message and honor for the methods, her eye for detail resulted in this unending conversation with Jesus.

- Thank you to Kathy Krenzien, Peyton Sepeda, James Reid, Caleb Jobe, and Cady Claterbaugh for overseeing the production and marketing of this project. Their faithful work made it possible to get this book into your hands!

To my prayer partners—my stick-closer-than-a brother-or-sister team—who always carry me over the finish line. *Always*. They pray for me with an unforced rhythm of grace and with boldness and confidence, believing in the ways God has invested prayer in me.

To Krista Doyle, my great-niece who lives out her own unique passion in prayer. She is a generational God-gift to me. Sharing our love of God and His Word and praying together has been one of my life's greatest joys.

To my prayer shield—Mallory and Boyd Bassham, Amy and Casey Cook, Stephanie and Allan Kelsey—who have been in the trenches and on the mountain tops with me these past eight years.

To Joan Byrne, my safe place and faithful soldier in prayer. How close we are in the spirit, even though we've only spoken once on the phone and met briefly one time. Oh, what God can do in agreeing prayer that miles cannot deter!

To Carol Sosa from Guatemala and her prayer team, who were impacted by my first book, *Adventures in Prayer*, and took on praying for this second project to come to pass.

To Christa Miles, Mark and Jodie Harris, Audrey Cook,

Monika Wiesinger, and Joanna Wiesinger, who wouldn't let me give up, shrink back, or quit. Living prayer with these wonderful friends is life's greatest gift!

To my wonderful sisters, Theresa and Raynora, who have known me longer than anyone else! And loved me, often in spite of myself. They have prayed and believed for me. They worry about me. They take care of me. With two sisters (Roberta and Bernadette) already in heaven, along with our parents, Theophil and Yula Mae Dobski, I can't say how much I treasure these two here on earth.

Lastly, though truly first and foremost, to my husband, Bruce Pierce—affectionally called Brucie. He is my Aaron and Hur partner in life. I love how he loves the Word as much as I do, and he is my most ardent supporter in what God wants to do in and through my prayer life. Brucie has made so many sacrifices for me. May God richly bless him and honor his legacy. Thirty-nine years married, and this is just our beginning.

As always, my greatest desire and prayer in writing is that this book will be a blessing and inspiration to my children, Toni and Traci, and my grandchildren, Mackenzie, Bethanie, Grant, Samantha, and Cassidy. And to the generations that will follow.

Loving God, following Jesus, being led by Holy Spirit, and living prayer is my dearest legacy to them.

ABOUT THE AUTHOR

Mary Jo Pierce has devoted nearly five decades to transforming lives through prayer and intercession. As a pastor, she pioneered innovative approaches to weave prayer into the fabric of church life, focusing on building people of prayer rather than just a prayer ministry. Her philosophy is simple yet profound: prayer isn't just something we do—it's fundamental to who we are.

Drawing from her extensive experience mentoring men, women, and young people, Mary Jo shares her passion for prayer through multiple creative outlets. Whether she's teaching classes, writing books and devotionals, taking pictures, sharing inspiration on social media, or baking bread, she consistently finds fresh ways to make prayer accessible and meaningful.

Mary Jo's books, *Adventures in Prayer* and *Let It Rise*, have inspired and unlocked the pure joy of living prayer and studying the Scriptures for thousands of people around the world.

Mary Jo resides in Keller, Texas, with her husband Bruce and their two "people from the Maltese tribe," Honor and Glory. Her greatest fulfillment comes from helping others discover the transformative power of an authentic prayer life. Connect with Mary Jo and explore her resources at maryjopierce.com.

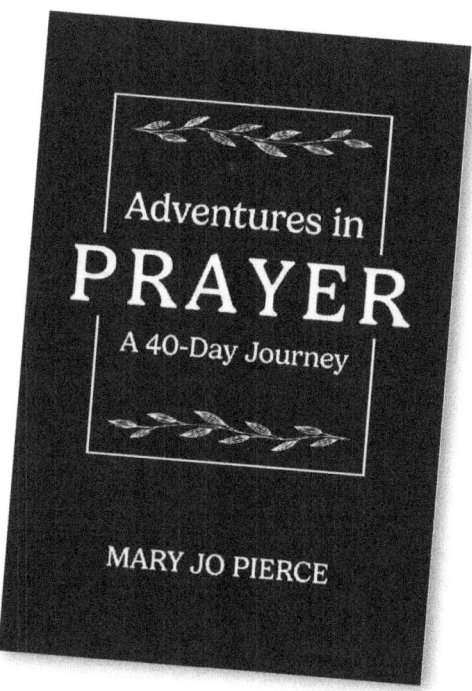

www.ingramcontent.com/pod-product-compliance
Lightning Source LLC
Chambersburg PA
CBHW060923120626
46557CB00003B/857